Be a Recruiting
SUPERSTAR

Charlene
29E Ra

Be a Recruiting
SUPERSTAR

The Fast Track to Network Marketing Millions

Mary Christensen

American Management Association

New York • Atlanta • Brussels • Chicago • Mexico City • San Francisco
Shanghai • Tokyo • Toronto • Washington, D.C.

Special discounts on bulk quantities of AMACOM books are available to corporations, professional associations, and other organizations. For details, contact Special Sales Department, AMACOM, a division of American Management Association, 1601 Broadway, New York, NY 10019.
Tel: 800-250-5308. Fax: 518-891-2372.
E-mail: specialsls@amanet.org
Website: www.amacombooks.org/go/specialsales
To view all AMACOM titles go to: www.amacombooks.org

This publication is designed to provide accurate and authoritative information in regard to the subject matter covered. It is sold with the understanding that the publisher is not engaged in rendering legal, accounting, or other professional service. If legal advice or other expert assistance is required, the services of a competent professional person should be sought.

Library of Congress Cataloging-in-Publication Data

Christensen, Mary, 1951–
    Be a recruiting superstar : the fast track to network marketing millions / Mary Christensen.
        p.   cm.
    Includes index.
    ISBN 978-0-8144-0163-7 (pbk.)
    1. Multilevel marketing.   2. Direct marketing.   I. Title.

HF5415.126.C48784   2008
658.8'72—dc22

                                                                        2007052952

Various names used by companies to distinguish their software and other products can be claimed as trademarks. AMACOM uses such names throughout this book for editorial purposes only, with no intention of trademark violation. All such software or product names are in initial capital letters or ALL CAPITAL letters. Individual companies should be contacted for complete information regarding trademarks and registration.

Printing number

10   9   8   7   6   5

This book is dedicated to my favorite people:

Ida, Ruby, Vera, Wayne, Nikki,

Matt, Paige, Trinity, David, Tiffany,

Samantha, Brayden, Dane, Beki,

Frances, Gary, Jim, Bev, Gordon,

Geoff, Catherine, Brittany, Callum,

Matt, Sonia, Grace, James, Jenny,

Mike, Tayla, Tristan, Caroline, Irian, Cayce,

Wayne, Tiffany, Mason, Marvon,

Kelly, Izak, Kaydence, and Bradley.

Contents

Foreword

IF YOU ARE IN THE network marketing business, start your own book club and make this your first selection and discuss it! Mary Christensen has created a clear, action-oriented how-to guide for building and developing a successful sales organization and a profitable business. Whether you are a newcomer to the network marketing industry or an experienced pro, the book is chock full of content that is easy to apply and works for anyone willing to devote the time and discipline to implementing the ideas.

The principles and techniques work regardless of the products or services sold or whether they are presented in a one-to-one selling situation, party-plan, or online. As promised in the title, the book provides a fast track to building a pipeline of salespeople and getting them inspired to follow your lead.

Mary clearly lays out for you the many advantages of a network marketing business and the broad appeal it offers to a variety of market segments, from twenty-somethings to active boomers and beyond. Recognizing that one size doesn't fit all, Mary helps you maximize your recruiting efforts by teaching you how to target the greatest number of prospects and how to build relationships with them from the first encounter. She also provides many samples of language to use and scripts to help you practice what you've learned.

Using Mary's humorous examples of bird species as a way to identify personality traits, you'll find yourself laughing out loud as you start to analyze friends, family, and team members. Whether prospects are peacocks, owls, doves, robins, or eagles, you'll learn how they can fit into your business, how to approach them, and how to keep them motivated. It's about learning what makes other people tick and recognizing that diversity will make your team stronger.

Ultimately, this book will help you identify what type of recruiter you are and how to advance from a star-in-the-making to a true recruiting superstar. Make this a must-read book to take ownership of the type of life you want to build.

—Betty Palm, President, Dove Chocolate at Home®

Be a Recruiting
SUPERSTAR

Introduction

DIRECT SELLING IS THE PERFECT WAY TO OWN A BUSINESS—and your life.

You can work with any products or services you choose, without worrying about production costs, inventory, or where you will source your goods. From skin care, nutritional supplements, and gourmet foods, to jewelry, toys, and pet care, the choices are overwhelming. Whatever your interests—gardening, wines, tea, coffee, or fashion—you'll be spoilt for choice.

Thousands of direct selling corporations are lining up to partner with you, with products and services including lingerie, leisurewear, telecommunications, health, travel, and legal services.

You can kiss good-bye demanding employers, office politics, and endless commutes. No more hours cooped up with people you may not like. You can choose when you work, where you work, and with whom you work.

If you have a business that is draining you both financially and emotionally, you can retire your loan, return the keys to the landlord, and partner with a corporation that will invest in you.

The corporation will subsidize your starter kit, provide sophisticated support systems, and train you at every level of your growth.

If you choose to work part-time, the income from your network marketing business is a simple way to top up the household budget for day-to-day expenses or for family treats. It can fund your kids' (or your own) college fees, pay for your family cruise to Alaska, and finance your home remodeling project.

A full-time network marketing business can generate enough income to support your family, pay off your mortgage, and build a plump retirement fund. It comes down to how much time you are prepared to work on your business and how willing you are to learn.

Recruiting is the life force of any network marketing, multi-level marketing, or party plan business. No matter how committed you are to promoting your products, there is a limit to how many people you can reach. Even if you are the greatest salesperson on the planet, there is a limit to the number of hours you can work. If you want to live a life most people only dream about, you have to learn to recruit.

Recruiting lifts the ceiling off your income. The way to reach the highest income levels is to find and train others to sell your product or services—and to teach them to do the same. Income generated from your personal sales, and the sales of everyone in your downline, can be your fast pass to financial freedom.

Residual income gives network marketing its edge. Like the royalties enjoyed by successful writers, singers, and actors, you continue to earn income after the groundwork is done. Even if you decide to cut back on your hours, the checks keep coming as long as you remain active and your people keep producing.

There are many reasons why network marketing is more popular than ever.

Consumers are growing immune to the barrage of mass advertising, celebrity endorsement, and spam. While traditional marketers are spending billions of dollars pushing their products through various media, network marketers are employing the most effective channel of all—word of mouth. The advertising budget is spent rewarding you.

As the pace of life speeds up, we all have less time to shop. Network marketing takes the hassle out of shopping because there are no crowded malls, jam-packed parking lots, or long lines at the checkout. Customers can choose how they shop—from a one-on-one consultation, home party, or business seminar, to ordering online or by phone. Their products will be delivered to their door, and repeat orders can be shipped automatically—with a generous loyalty discount attached.

For retail shoppers, service is fast becoming extinct. Retailers are cutting their overheads by hiring low-paid, low-skilled workers. By contrast, the majority of network marketers are highly trained and motivated. Their income and lifestyles depend on it.

The novelty of shoddy goods sold from tacky discount stores and unsightly retail barns has worn off. More than a few scares over safety issues have cooled our desire for cheap imports. Quality products that are backed by satisfaction guarantees are the hallmarks of network marketing.

Customers are fed up with the "We don't care, you don't matter" approach adopted by so-called service providers. We dislike our calls being answered by robots. We resent being put on hold while being assured, "Your call is important to us," at the same time. It's no wonder network marketers who compete with high-end products and personal services are gaining ground.

Network marketing is an incredible opportunity for anyone looking to start his or her own business. Your income is determined by how skilled you are at finding the right people and giving them the support they need to build their organizations. Your recruits immediately have the same income opportunities you have. It's the ultimate equal opportunity business.

If you are serious about building a network marketing organization and reaping the high rewards earned by the stars of the industry, recruiting must be your number-one priority. Less than

1 percent of the world's population is currently involved in direct selling. Spell that P-O-T-E-N-T-I-A-L!

This book will teach you the innovative approach to recruiting I developed to fast-track my own business. I will help you take the guesswork out of recruiting by showing you *who* your best prospects are and where to find them. I will explain *why* they are a perfect fit for your opportunity and *how* to make your approach. None of it is complicated. Ask the right questions and you will have your hottest prospects identifying themselves.

There are already well over 15 million people involved in network marketing in the United States and more than 60 million worldwide. One in every ten households has someone involved in direct selling. New people are flocking to the industry in staggering numbers. Every day, twenty-five thousand new representatives join in the United States and more than eighty thousand sign on worldwide.

There are countless reasons why those numbers will continue to escalate in the years ahead, starting with technological advancements that allow anyone to run a small, home-based business with resources that equal any large corporation's.

The Internet has transformed the business of direct selling. It liberates network marketers from tasks that consume time, such as sending customer newsletters, making deliveries, and tracking personal and team sales. Greater efficiency at the back-end of the business frees you to focus on front-end activities that produce income.

As traditional jobs are swallowed up by automation or drift offshore, workers are realizing the only security in life is self-reliance. The term *offshore* is not a threatening word in network marketing. It is an opportunity to spread your network into new countries, especially the developing markets of Russia, India, China, and Eastern and Central Europe.

Any savvy businessperson knows that bricks and mortar do not make a business. People make a business. The greatest advantage of a network marketing business is the minimal cost to start and maintain it. You don't have to rent premises or buy inventory. You don't have to borrow money. You pay as you go and you earn as you learn.

☆ ☆ ☆ ☆ ☆

I started in network marketing with an abundance of confidence in the vision of the corporation, its one-of-a-kind products, and what to my eyes seemed to be an incredible opportunity. Armed with an arsenal of superlatives I set out on a mission to sell the business to anyone who crossed my path.

The mission failed. Sure, I sold a few products and signed up a few friends and neighbors. But, like so many others who start out with starry eyes and a flawed strategy, I wasn't earning enough to survive full-time as I had hoped when I resigned my teaching job.

Determined to be a stay-at-home mom and pay the bills, I decided to give myself another chance. Clearly, I had to find a better way to run my business.

I changed my strategy and the results were instantaneous. I started tapping into people's lives instead of subjecting them to a torrent of information they may or may not be interested in. My sales and recruiting skyrocketed.

I earned enough to repay my mortgage, buy a new home, drive my dream car, and take my children on vacations halfway around the world. I could afford to give them one of the greatest gifts of all—a quality education without the burden of student debt. At a young age, I was debt-free, with an investment portfolio that gave me the freedom to live the life I chose—and the money to pay for it.

If I can do it, so can you, because I know how few skills and what little confidence I had when I started out. I saw myself as the Thomas Edison of network marketing—learning a thousand ways that didn't work before I discovered one that did.

When you are ready to transfer your dreams from your wish list to your to-do list, I will show you how to master the art of recruiting so that you can build a profitable network marketing or party plan business. If you are willing to work and willing to learn, you too can have the money—*and* your life.

> Sell products and you will earn money for now. Recruit
> and you will earn money forever.
>
> —MARY CHRISTENSEN

PART I

Prepare to Recruit

CHAPTER ONE

Why People Become Network Marketers and Why They Don't

HERE ARE TWO SIMPLE QUESTIONS.

First, what is the number-one reason people start a network marketing or party plan business?

The answer is that they started the business because someone asked them. The overwhelming majority of people never considered the business before they were approached.

That is not surprising. Our business is word of mouth. We don't run media campaigns trumpeting our opportunity and we don't advertise in the job opportunities section of the newspaper. Unless and until you connect with your prospects, how will they know how incredible the opportunity is?

Second, what is the number-one reason people *don't* start a network marketing or party plan business?

And the answer is that nobody asked them! People are not going to come knocking on your door. You have to reach out to them—preferably before someone else does. Believe me, there will be no harsher lesson than seeing someone you could have approached, but didn't, turn up at a corporate event as someone else's star recruit.

Every day, thousands of people who never seriously considered a network marketing business sign an agreement. Luckily for them, they were in the right place at the right time when the right person came along. That person could be you.

Don't prejudge, don't hesitate, and don't hold back. Approach people and talk about the business at every opportunity you get. If an opportunity doesn't present itself, create one. The more people you talk to, the more successful you will be.

All you need is a belief in your products, your opportunity, and courage.

If you have not yet done so, choosing your products will be the easy part. Just about every product now is sold directly. Iconic brands like Avon, which has been in business for more than 120 years, are being joined by household brands like Dove Chocolate®, Jockey®, and The Body Shop® that have traditionally sold retail. Choose a product you can be passionate about and a corporation with a genuine desire to serve you.

No matter how great your products or how much support you get from your corporate partner, your success will be up to you. So, here is the million-dollar question: How much success do you think you deserve? If you don't think you deserve success, you'll find a thousand excuses why it won't happen for you, such as "I'm too young, old, busy, not confident or smart enough, not a salesperson . . ."

Read between the lines and what you really are saying is, "I'm too (busy) so don't expect me to (try)." You're giving yourself a free pass to fail, but "stinking thinking" always comes at a price.

Here is something else to think about. What if you do have what it takes to create an amazing life from your network marketing business, and then give up without giving it your best shot?

There is no penalty for not reaching your goals, so what do

you have to lose? Go for it and you may surprise yourself by achieving success beyond your wildest dreams. Give yourself permission to succeed—and to succeed spectacularly. Tell yourself, a thousand times if that is what it takes to believe it, "I want it, I deserve it, and I can do it."

To put yourself out there every day takes courage, and you will almost certainly face a few setbacks. This is when you have to make a choice—to pull into an emotionally handicapped space and stay parked or to drive on regardless. As the famed American writer Mark Twain said in *Pudd'nhead Wilson*, "Courage is resistance to fear, mastery of fear—not absence of fear."

If you wait to become confident before you start recruiting, you will waste your best opportunities. Confidence will come once you see the positive impact you can make on others.

If you wait until you have an encyclopedic knowledge of your compensation plan, it may be a long wait. Skills come from practice. The only way to learn to play the guitar is, well, to play the guitar.

It takes courage to build a network marketing business. No matter how nervous you feel, reach out to as many people as you can. Encourage every person you recruit to do the same.

Don't buy into the fiction you don't have what it takes to succeed. Or that it's difficult to find the right people. Or that something may go wrong. If you want it—and believe you deserve it—you can do it.

There are 300 million people living in the United States. A new person is born every seven seconds, and an immigrant enters the country every fourteen seconds. Very few people are living the life of their dreams. You may hold the key. Find the courage to reach out to people every day, knowing you have the power to change lives.

If you lack confidence at the start, turn it to your advantage. Knowing exactly how your new recruits feel when they start out will make you an empathetic leader. When you say, "I know how you feel, I felt the same way," you will be speaking from the heart.

A leader who says, "I am still learning too," is a more powerful role model than one who appears flawless. The message you will be communicating is, "If I can do this, you can too."

Put yourself in a room of network marketing achievers and you won't immediately spot an obvious common denominator. Every socioeconomic background, education level, profession, job, ethnicity, race, gender, personality, and age will be represented. You have to look beneath the surface to see what they have in common, which is a belief in the business, the ambition to succeed, and the courage to make it happen.

You can be whoever you want to be, have whatever you want to have, do whatever you want to do. What better way to realize your dreams than to build a party plan or network marketing organization by one person at a time?

CHAPTER TWO

Recruiting Principles That Will Transform Your Business

THERE ARE TWO WAYS TO RECRUIT. The first is to approach everyone you know and everyone you meet, hoping each will have enough kindness, politeness, or patience to hear you out!

I call it the *ambush* technique. It is tough on your unsuspecting prospect and it is tough on you, because—surprise—the rejection rate is high. That is because you come across like you're trying to help yourself by convincing others to consider your business opportunity.

The second way is decide *before* you start calling *whom* you are looking for and *why* this person may be interested in your opportunity. You're looking for a *connect*. When you approach people you know are right for the business, your prospects will see that you genuinely believe you have something to offer them. Always be ready to say, "I called you because . . ."

Will they join? Maybe they will, maybe they won't. Many factors will influence your prospects' decision. You can only control how well you approach them, not how they respond. But one thing is guaranteed: Approach prospects with a genuine desire to help them and you will dramatically increase your success rate. Even if they decline your opportunity, the door will stay open.

You will get a better response if you understand and adopt the following key principles.

Principle Number One

Find a need and fill it.

Imagine your prospect is a target, and all the benefits of your opportunity are arrows. Ready to start firing those arrows?

But wait—before you take aim, you're going to be blindfolded. Once you are blindfolded, your prospect can move anywhere he or she wants. If you don't know where your prospect is standing, you won't know where to aim. My guess is that none of your arrows will reach their target.

You are probably thinking, "What a big waste of time!" And you are right. There is no point in firing random arrows if you can't see your target. You have to know where your prospects stand *before* you start trying to sell them on your opportunity. It's called listening.

If you spend 80 percent of your time learning about your prospects' ambitions, experiences, personality, circumstances, and priorities, you won't waste your time or theirs shooting arrows that don't apply to or interest them. The 20 percent of time you spend talking will be right on target.

Principle Number Two

Duplication!

The way to fast-track your business is to reach out to as many people as possible. The more people you approach, the more people will join and the faster you will build your organization.

Imagine you want to recruit a thousand people into your downline (the people you recruit and train and from whose sales you also earn a commission). What if you recruit one person a month? How long will it take to recruit one thousand? It will take eighty-three years! At best, you'll be enjoying the rewards of your labor from a motorized mobility scooter.

What about one person a week? You'll be busy, but in just about twenty years, you'll reach your target. That's a little behind schedule if one of your goals is to fund your kids' college educations. They'll have joined the 30 percent of students who are forced to drop out due to financial hardship or who graduated with a hefty student loan long before you reach your college fund target.

What if you taught every person you recruited to recruit, and each one did the same? How long would it take to bring a thousand people into your downline? It would take ten months! Not eighty-three years, not twenty years, just ten months!

If you want to build your organization fast, your approach to recruiting has to be easy to learn, remember, and repeat. You may have superpowers or a unique strategy that works for you personally, but the more you stray from the tried-and-true system, the harder it will be to replicate your example. If you want to be duplicable, you can't afford to do anything others can't copy.

Principle Number Three

The more you say, the less they will hear.

Words will not convince people to buy your products or your opportunity. The more time you spend talking, the less time they will spend listening. The faster you talk, the more desperate you will sound.

Information overload has become a national epidemic. The volume of information we must process every day is staggering, with researchers suggesting we are bombarded with five thousand messages a day. We cope by filtering out unnecessary, irrelevant, or unwanted information, tuning in only when we're interested, and tuning out when we're not. If you want your message to be heard over the clutter, you have to make every word count.

Politicians, lobbyists, and business leaders know that the punchier the sound bite, the more likely it is to be picked up by the media. Marketers know they have mere seconds to reach consumers in commercials. There is a direct link between simplicity and impact—the more you say, the less they'll hear.

People are a little like water. We tend to follow the easiest route. Every complication, every unnecessary detail, gives us an excuse to say, "No," or "Not now." Don't be heavy-handed. Make it easy for prospects to make a positive decision by keeping it simple.

The clearer your message, the better the odds that your recruits will relay it intact to the people they recruit. It takes discipline and practice to be brief, but it works.

Principle Number Four

It's not about you.

Imagine that you've had a tough day and the pressure is mounting. Friends are coming to dinner and you have two hours to drive across town, collect the kids from Little League, and fix a meal before they arrive.

The traffic is heavy, the thermometer is pushing 90 degrees, and the kids are tired and fractious. You restore harmony with the promise of pizza and a DVD (now you're feeling stressed and guilty) and head for the supermarket.

You've performed this drill many times. A quick circuit of the market and you will emerge with everything you need to be the perfect host.

The parking lot is packed. A car guarding a pending space is blocking an entire line of traffic. The clock is ticking. You finally nab a parking space at the far end of the lot and race in the heat to the market. As you head for the carts, you come face-to-face with the store greeter.

"Thank you for choosing to shop at Walker's fresh food market!" she says brightly.

"Thanks," you reply, tugging at the cart.

She continues, "We hope you enjoy your shopping experience with us today."

You're wasting precious seconds, but you don't want to be impolite. You force a smile.

"It's our tenth anniversary," the greeter says, "and we are celebrating with some fabulous specials. Here are your coupons." She thrusts a pamphlet into your hands.

"Thanks." You force a smile and reach once more for the cart.

"You're very welcome," she says, oblivious to your only wish—a record-breaking circuit of the store. "We have some in-store promotions today that may interest you."

You decide to bypass the cart for the handbasket, but your escape route is blocked.

"Our founder's vision . . ."

You sense your kids are about to start World War III behind your back.

". . . is to stock only the freshest meat and produce."

"Sorry," you interrupt, as your blood pressure rises, "But I'm in a rush."

If your tormentor hears you, it doesn't register. "Make sure you drop by the delicatessen," she smiles "and sample our delicious new cheeses."

Aargh! The greeter is bursting with enthusiasm—and being totally insensitive to your needs.

The store has one agenda, which is to capitalize on its anniversary to promote the store. You have another agenda, which is to complete your shopping experience in as short a time as possible. Had the greeter read your signals, she would have stepped back to allow you to sprint past.

When it comes to promoting your business, it must always be about your prospects. Their agendas will be different from yours and different from the prospect you talked with yesterday.

One size doesn't fit all. You have to approach every call, every interview, and every presentation from your prospect's perspective. Haranguing your prospects about the founder's vision or company mission will slash your chances of turning them into recruits.

I can only begin you tell you how many times I've watched from the back of an opportunity meeting as the audience switched off halfway through a lecture on the compensation plan or visuals of the home office. I've attended countless parties where an eager but misguided distributor fired random shots over the heads of guests who may have been hot prospects.

It's easier to talk about your products and opportunity than to venture into uncertain territory—your prospect's unique circumstances—but it is a huge mistake.

The time for details is at training. Prospecting is the time to connect with your prospects and for them to connect with you. The fastest way to connect is to show a genuine interest in your prospect's life. Ask about the person's family and friends. Find out where the person's passions lie, or what the person does in his or her spare time, or where the person works and where he or she went to college. When you show you are interested in the prospect, he or she will be interested in you.

Principle Number Five

Emotion carries more weight than logic.

People are driven by emotion, not logic. We base our decisions on our feelings, and then we justify them with reason. If your approach is too theoretical, rational, or dry, you will drive people away. Belief and passion will inspire your prospects.

Here is how one former nurse who became a party planner tells her story at parties:

> I was at work when the phone rang. It was my son's baby-sitter and she said, "Your baby just turned over for the first time." All I could think of was that I wasn't there when it happened. In that second I decided to resign my job to be home with my son.

After hearing her story, every parent in the room experiences an immediate, emotional, instinctive reaction. If you want to touch hearts, then you must speak from the heart.

Principle Number Six

Build relationships.

The day you started your network marketing business, you started a career in the relationship business. Take away the relationship aspect of network marketing and nothing separates you from any other retailer, direct marketer, or online seller.

Your products or services may be superb, but it's naïve to believe yours are the only quality products on the market.

Your remuneration plan may be amazing, your home office staff willing to go to any lengths to serve you, but there are other corporations with a great plans and great staff.

Your training programs and support system may be state-of-the-art. But with fast-moving advances in technology, any corporation can develop outstanding support materials.

The only thing that cannot be copied, or imitated, is your relationship with others. You will waste all the time, effort, and energy you spend on finding prospects if you neglect to build relationships with them. Prospects sign with people they like and they stay with people they like.

Take advantage of technological innovations to build and manage your organization, but never become so high-tech that you neglect the high-touch approach that is the magic of network marketing.

Principle Number Seven

Work the numbers.

Not everyone you approach will join, and not everyone will stay. Most will join with small goals; others will join because they are intent on reaching the top ranks of the business. A few will have what it takes to make it happen, while others will be dreamers who lack the determination and discipline required.

You need to approach lots of people. Work your business like a numbers game if you want to join the top income earners, because that is how it works.

Principle Number Eight

It's never too soon to start.

The sooner you start recruiting, the sooner you will get results. You may struggle with the thought of recruiting when you're new. But think for a moment about when you are most excited about anything. When it's new, of course! Enthusiasm carries more weight than details. Don't waste that positive energy. Channel your excitement into recruits by telling everyone what you are doing and why you are doing it, right from the start.

If you are thinking, "I don't know enough yet about the business. I don't want to make an idiot of myself if someone asks me a question I can't answer," then my advice is to relax.

There is nothing wrong with answering, "I don't know, but I'll find out," to questions you can't answer. It gives you a reason to call back. Or you might say, "I'm still getting the hang of it.

Why don't you come to a training meeting and take a first-hand look at the business?"

There are many ways to introduce a prospect to the business and a wealth of resources you can call on for help. Some companies encourage new representatives to involve their sponsors or managers in the interview. Others recommend three-way calls, DVDs, CDs, telecasts, or webcasts to tell the story.

Whatever you do, don't let inexperience or insecurity stop you recruiting from day one. The sooner you start, the sooner your first person will sign. Nothing builds confidence like success, and you will have more credibility when you challenge your newcomers to overcome their recruiting-reluctance roadblock.

Principle Number Nine

Recruit with integrity.

Hype is the number-one enemy of this business. Have you ever been tempted by an advertisement for a product that seemed almost too good to be true? When it turned out to be a dud, you felt annoyed and betrayed. But the last laugh is yours because you will never do business with that company again and you will broadcast your disappointment out loud.

If you tell me I can make $20,000 a month within six months, you will have one disillusioned puppy on your hands when it doesn't happen.

Enthusiasm is no excuse for exaggerating or misrepresenting the effort required to build a business or the rewards that can be earned. It takes time, commitment, and a willingness to learn to become a top income earner.

If you back your belief in your opportunity with realistic explanations and a genuine desire to help your prospects, you will build a stable organization of people who understand that rewards follow results. Your value-packed opportunity does not need embellishing.

Principle Number Ten

Lead by example.

You can't expect others to do what you do not. The highest income earners in the business are pacesetters. They sell and recruit consistently and they expect the people they recruit to do the same.

After they build impressive organizations, they avoid the trap of managing rather than leading. They know the activities that took them to the top will keep them there.

Make a commitment to recruit more people than anyone else in your organization—and do this every month. Shoot for every recruiting incentive your corporate partner offers. Not only will you enjoy more rewards and more recognition but you will also earn respect as a leader who leads from the front.

CHAPTER THREE

How to Connect with More People

YOU ARE EITHER A GOOD or a bad advertisement for your business. People judge you by your appearance, and their response can be positive or negative. There is no neutral. If they don't notice you, that is a major negative. You want to make an impression that invites people to spend time with you talking about the business.

Imagine you are an actor auditioning for a role. You have only a few seconds to warm the casting director to you, so you must think carefully about what you will wear and how you will walk, talk, and act to make an outstanding impression the moment you walk on stage.

Imagine you are a doctor. Winning your patients' trust is a critical part of the doctor/patient relationship. Wearing the mantle of your profession takes you a long way toward earning that trust.

Every day we play a variety of personal roles—mother, father, wife, husband, son, daughter, grandparent, neighbor, and friend. We go to work and become a manager, employee, service provider, representative, assistant, adviser, supervisor, teacher, or caregiver. We switch from one role to another several times a day, and in most cases we do it instinctively.

Network marketing is no different. The roles you will play as your organization grows almost certainly will include talent scout, headhunter, trainer, coach, mentor, cheerleader, seller, and administrator. If you think like a professional, you'll stand out as a professional.

The better your image, the more likely it is you will attract the right people. Think about the qualities you want to convey.

First, you want to look successful, because you are promoting success. If you are starting out, project an image of the success you will become. Don't let money stop you. When I started out, I lived in one suit until I could afford a new one. My car was ancient, but it was clean.

Do your clothes convey success? Are they in style? Is your handshake firm? Is your grooming immaculate? Is your voice confident?

You want to look approachable so that people feel comfortable around you. Do you smile frequently and make eye contact easily? Do you hold the door for the person behind you? Are you courteous to people you meet regardless of who they are, how well you know them, or how "important" they are? Do you take every opportunity to say, "Thank you"? Are you a generous tipper?

You want to look happy and relaxed because if you radiate pressure, tension, and stress, you portray a negative image of yourself and the business. No one will want to join a business that adds to his or her stress level. Do you turn off your cell phone when you are with company? Do you give people your full attention, instead of allowing your eyes to dart around the room? Do you laugh often? Are you always *on* or can you switch to *off* when you are not working?

You never know when or where you will meet your next prospect, so always be prepared. Advertise your pride in your products by using them at every opportunity. Make sure your home is brimming with evidence of your passion. Give your products as gifts. Your sincerity will be reflected in what you do, not what you say.

If you are selling healthcare products, you will have more credibility if you project an aura of well-being. If your products promise weight loss, do you have before-and-after photos to show? If you are a work in progress, do you walk tall and wear clothes that complement your body shape?

If your business is skin care and cosmetics, does your skin glow with vitality? Is your makeup fresh and fashionable? Is it appropriate for your age?

If you represent clothing or jewelry, do you dress to impress? Do you wear colors that suit your skin tone? Do your accessories attract compliments?

Your voice communicates a powerful message to prospects. Do you convey enthusiasm and credibility or insecurity and insincerity? Does your speech rate come across as stressed and anxious or calm and confident? Are you concise and clear or rambling and long-winded? Will your prospects sense your genuine interest in their opinions? Do you listen to their answers without interruptions?

When you look, talk, and act the part, wherever you are in your business development, you will both look and feel more confident. Your prospects will pick up on your self-assurance.

Image is more than your personal demeanor. You have a competitive advantage in the first-class business materials produced by your corporate partner. Work that advantage. Don't produce your own materials or make copies to save a few dollars, and don't deface brochures with shoddy personalization.

Buy the best-quality business cards and stationery you can afford and use simple, contemporary graphics. A simple, clean business card will look more professional than a cluttered one. Never be caught out having to say, "I don't have any cards with me right now."

Get the basics right. Avoid fancy typefaces that can look ama-

teurish. Spell-check and proofread your communications before
you click "send." Carry your demonstration products in professional carry-cases and discard worn stock. Handle and display
your products with pride.

Above all—and I cannot stress this point enough—take every
opportunity to demonstrate pride in your business. When people
ask about your job, make sure the first words out of your mouth
express your pride.

> "I'm a network marketer. I work from home selling top-of-the-
> line herbal supplements."
>
> "I sell pure essential oils at home parties."
>
> "I'm a party planner. I demonstrate and sell chocolate at home
> parties."
>
> "I'm in network marketing. I have my own business marketing
> a range of leisurewear."
>
> "I am an independent distributor for a party plan company that
> sells natural body-care products."

Your confidence and enthusiasm will be infectious. Even
when you become a manager, describing your job from a distributor's perspective will make it easier to start conversations with
potential recruits.

You have made it easy for them to say, "I have a friend who
works with . . ." or "What company do you work with?"

Too many network marketers offer confusing or glib explanations about the business they are in, such as, "I'm in the business
of empowering people." Say, what? Or worse, they say, "I help
people make money!" Tacky.

If you are not excited about what you do, how can you expect
others to be?

CHAPTER FOUR

How Much Do You Know About Network Marketing?

MYOPIA IS A NICE PLACE TO VISIT, but you can't afford to live there. Perhaps your company is the greatest ever, but you will connect with more prospects if you have a wider knowledge of the business and can answer questions confidently. Here are the must-know basics of the business:

    *   Whether you are a party planner or a network or multi-level marketer, you are in the business of direct selling. Direct selling describes the sale of goods and services direct to the consumer rather than from a fixed retail location.

    *   The global direct selling market exceeds $110 billion in sales per year.

    *   The United States is the largest at over $32 billion, with Japan in second place at $25 billion. Mexico and France exceed $3 billion. Direct selling is strong in Canada, Australia, Europe, and South America. With their massive populations, Asia, India,

Russia, and China are emerging markets with mind-boggling potential.

⋆ Just about every product or service imaginable is available through direct selling channels. Home products—such as cleaning, cookware, home decor, foods, and pet care—account for the largest share at 33.5 percent. Personal care products—such as skin care, cosmetics, fragrances, and jewelry—come in second place at 28.2 percent. Services—such as financial, travel, and communications—contribute 15.5 percent. Wellness products, which include nutritional supplements, beverages, and weight-loss products, add 15.4 percent. Leisure and educational products contribute 7.4 percent.

⋆ Four out of five direct sellers are women, and 10 percent of businesses are run as partnerships, primarily by married couples.

⋆ From a business and tax perspective, direct sellers are classified as independent, self-employed operators or contractors, although they use a variety of titles such as representatives, distributors, associates, stylists, coordinators, consultants, specialists, advisers, or business owners. Their income comes from commissions, bonuses, and overrides on personal and group sales, typically on an escalating scale. The higher their sales, the higher the percentage they earn.

⋆ Network marketing (also known as multilevel marketing) is an extension of direct selling. While *direct selling* refers to how products are sold, *network* or *multilevel* marketing refers to how you are paid for building your organization.

⋆ In addition to being paid on your sales, you earn income on the sales of people you recruit (or enroll, introduce, or sponsor) into the business. This includes both direct recruits (people you personally recruit) and indirect recruits (people recruited by the people you recruit). Both direct and indirect recruits belong in your downline organization.

⋆ The term *width* is used to describe people you personally recruit (your first levels), and the term *depth* is used to describe people recruited by your first levels (and your second levels, third levels, etc.).

★ The term *leg* describes the genealogy of your recruits—that is, the people recruited downline from each of your first levels.

★ The higher your rank on the compensation plan, the higher the percentage you earn on your recruits.

★ Every contractor who signs a direct selling, network marketing, or party plan agreement is paid directly by the corporation. The payments are outlined in a compensation plan (sometimes known as a marketing plan). Most of these plans are written by brainiacs more skilled at calculating numbers than communicating them. If you find your plan confusing, don't assume you are stupid. Do what the rest of us do and ask someone to translate it into English for you.

★ But here is where it gets exciting: approximately 50 percent of the revenue from products sold is available as commissions—to you and the people you recruit and train.

★ How can network marketing corporations afford to redistribute half of their revenue while maintaining the quality and integrity of their products? That's easy. Whereas traditional marketers rely on media advertising, sponsorships, and celebrity endorsements to promote their products and services (think $2,500,000 for just *one* thirty-second commercial during the Super Bowl), network marketing corporations pay you to share your experience, belief, and enthusiasm in your products with others.

★ There is more. Unlike hapless retailers who must buy and store products to sell, network marketers carry little or no inventory. The corporation takes care of production, packaging, inventory, and shipping. Many corporations ship directly to your customers, freeing you to spend more time doing what you are paid to do, which is to sell products and recruit and train others to do the same. Many corporations auto-ship to customers on a regular cycle. You still get paid for these sales.

✶   Direct sellers do not have to worry about the cost of returns or exchanges. If a product is unsatisfactory or damaged, the corporation is responsible for refunds or replacements.

Occasionally you will come across a prospect who is confused about the difference between network marketing and pyramid selling. In a nutshell, network marketing is a legitimate business activity, while pyramid selling is not.

Pyramid schemes (or Ponzi schemes) encourage and reward people for recruiting when there is little or no value in the products and services. They are illegal because they entice the unwary, unwitting, and unwise into a scheme that will most likely lose them money. Nevertheless, they pop up from time to time, so it will help if you can identify them.

Some schemes are presented as games to trap the unwary. For example, there is the airplane game, where participants were encouraged to sell "seats" in an imaginary "airplane." Once you fill your "airplane," you collect the money, while those who bought "seats" have to fill their own planes. It sounds nonsensical, and it is, which only proves some people are suckers.

The offering of so-called collector items that are priced much higher than their true value is another scheme designed to make the originators rich at the expense of everyone else.

Any scheme that encourages participants to buy large amounts of product (called *front-end loading*), which usually end up in basements and garages unsold, is considered a pyramid.

Pyramid schemes tempt greedy, lazy, and naïve people with high commissions and bonuses, which is often based on how much product is bought at the entry level. If it seems too good to be true, it probably is. Both the originators and the participants of these Ponzi schemes can expect to end up in jail.

✶ ✶ ✶ ✶ ✶ ✶

In a genuine network marketing or party plan business, all rewards are based on sales. If someone you recruit doesn't sell, you earn nothing. Regardless of how many people you recruit, you won't get paid unless—and until—they sell products.

What you earn on the sales of your recruits is your reward for finding, training, and supporting them, just as any professional is paid for leadership responsibilities. This does not affect what your recruits earn, and they have exactly the same opportunity as you to build their own organization.

The more you know about your products and your business opportunity, the better equipped you will be to promote them. Your corporation will have a wealth of print copy or downloadable information on your products and opportunity. You will have access to conventions, meetings, and seminars, as well as tele-training and Web training. Your upline (or sponsor)—that is, the person who recruited you—also may be a rich source of hands-on knowledge.

This book focuses on recruiting. If you are looking for help in building your organization, I recommend reading *Be a Network Marketing Superstar*, which offers a step-by-step guide to success. You can order it from my website (www.marychristensen.com), where you can also find information on live seminars coming to your area, conference calls, and how to sign up for my e-zine.

Knowledge brings credibility. When your confidence in your unique opportunity is based on a wider perspective of the industry, you will connect with more prospects.

> If I had to live my life over again, I would elect to be a trader of goods
> rather than a student of science.
>
> —Albert Einstein

CHAPTER FIVE

Assemble Your Tools

YOU NEVER KNOW WHEN you will meet your next prospect, so always have sponsoring tools with you and make sure you are ready to seize every opportunity that presents itself.

Don't be heavy-handed. Sort through the materials your corporate partner offers before choosing what you relate to best. Dumping a surfeit of information on prospects will not help your cause.

You should carry the following basic tools with you at all times:

✴ Business cards. These are essential. Make them simple and make sure they describe what you do—for example, *Independent distributor of [. . .] home spa products*. You may like to add a conversation starter if you have the personality to carry it off, such as, "Free consultations on how to turn your spare room into a profitable business" or "Be paid to lose weight/train as a fashion coordinator/herb specialist/chocolatier."

✴ Copies of any newspaper or magazine articles featuring

your company. These third-party support materials such as magazines, newspapers, CDs, and DVDs add to your credibility. Several independent publishers specialize in creating support materials for network marketers. Preview them before you invest, because the style, content, and quality can vary.

✶ Brochures advertising incentives such as a cruise to the Caribbean. Enticing promotions introduce an element of urgency and can turn a wavering prospect into a committed recruit.

✶ An overview of the compensation plan. An abbreviated version is better than the full plan, as a plan chock-full of confusing industryspeak can frighten prospects away.

✶ Details of upcoming opportunity meetings or training seminars. Have invitations printed that specify to bring a partner/friend. Include an RSVP.

✶ Agreements with your name and representative ID number filled out and ready to sign.

✶ A starter kit unpacked from its shipping box. A drab cardboard box will not excite a prospect, nor will layers of recycled paper and foam chips. Display your starter kit in an attractive container, and bind your literature in a folder that you can easily flip through.

✶ A pack of your key products so that interested prospects can try the products immediately. Say, "Would you like to try the products? These are the most popular and they normally retail for $60. Because I appreciate your meeting with me, I will give them to you for $50." (Now you have created a reason to stay in touch, by asking prospects, "How did you enjoy the products?")

✶ An up-to-date bullet-point list detailing the benefits and current incentives your new recruit will receive on signing. Create it on your PC so that you can update it as new promotions and incentives are introduced. Every benefit will increase the perceived value of the starter kit, and different benefits will appeal to different prospects, so list them all.

Here's an example you can adapt to fit your needs.

1. A selection of our best-selling products worth over $600!
2. A comprehensive training manual.
3. Enough literature and stationery for your first month in business.
4. A full-day seminar on how to start your business.
5. Training telecasts or (Web seminars) every month.
6. A free gift valued at $50 when you place your first order within thirty days!
7. A gift worth $75 for introducing a friend in your first sixty days!
8. A subscription to a monthly magazine.
9. Your own website—the first month is free and after that you pay just a $[. . .] service fee a month.
10. Direct online access to the company website for news, updates, events, and special online-only offers.
11. Direct access to your own personal sales and recruiting results.
12. An invitation every year to the annual convention (this year it's in Las Vegas).
13. The chance to receive a free vacation (this year it's in the Bahamas).
14. Your own personal business coach. That's me! I'm here to give you all the support you need.
. . . All for an investment of $300!

★ P.S. Don't forget your planner. No appointments, no business!

CHAPTER SIX

Develop Your Personal Success Story

THE BEST TOOL YOU HAVE to promote your business is you. Every-one prefers real-life experiences to lectures, and when you share your story, people will listen. These true stories are testimony to the power of personal experience.

David's Story

When a driver ran a red light and smashed into his car, David's hands were so badly burned, his career as a graphic designer was destroyed in an instant.

Although doctors advised skin grafts to repair the damage, a friend recommended David first try a new range of healing skin products. Facing months of expensive, painful surgery, David decided he had nothing to lose.

Several times a day he massaged the balm into his hands. To document his progress and to keep his spirits up, his wife took photos. As the wounds healed and new skin grew beneath the scars, it became obvious surgery was unnecessary.

The photos created an outstanding testimonial for the products. David was so impressed that he started selling the products himself and soon developed a thriving business. To introduce new people to his opportunity, he shows the photos and lets the evidence speak for itself.

Angela's Story

An avid beach volleyball player, Angela practically lived in the sun in her teens and twenties. By age forty, she was paying for it. Depressing brown blotches were appearing on her face, chest, and arms.

At first Angela tried covering the spots with makeup, but that made her skin look dull and masklike.

Angela's dermatologist recommended a skin-care program to fade the blotches and protect her skin from further sun damage. Within weeks, the blotches had disappeared and Angela's skin looked fresh and glowing again.

Angela is now a leading distributor for the products.

Catherine's Story

When Catherine heard about her high-school reunion, her excitement quickly turned to dread. When she last saw her classmates she was a size six and captain of the cheerleading team. Now she weighed 180 pounds.

After a sleepless night, Catherine decided if there was ever a time to do something about her weight, this was it. She called a friend who had recently become a weight-loss consultant and signed up on the spot. Every day, she replaced two meals with a nutritionally balanced shake and most days she walked for at least thirty minutes. As hard as it was to stay focused, she lost ten pounds in less than a month.

When friends saw how great she was looking, everyone wanted to know her secret. Catherine quickly spotted the potential in sharing her experience and decided to start selling the program herself. Not only could she buy her own products cheaper, she made enough money to buy a whole new wardrobe.

Catherine attended her high-school reunion weighing thirty pounds lighter and wearing clothes she never dreamed she could afford. Several former classmates commented on how great she looked.

To promote her business, Catherine carries three photos with her—the "fat" photo she took the day she started the program, her class reunion photo, and a photo taken in Hawaii on a trip she earned for her sales, wearing a bright red size-six swimsuit.

★ ★ ★ ★ ★ ★

Real-life experiences always are more persuasive than facts, figures, and statistics. The more vivid the picture you paint, the more powerful your story.

If your story is not dramatic, you can create a powerful testimonial with thought and preparation. Start developing your story by answering the following questions:

* Why did you start using the products?
* What changed when you started using the products?
* What were you doing before you started your business?
* What prompted you to start your business?
* What doubts did you have?
* How were they resolved?
* What challenges did you have?
* How did you overcome them?
* How has your life changed since you started your business?

* What experiences have you had as a direct result of your business?

* How has your business affected your family?

If it seems too soon to build your story, perhaps the following questions will help:

* What difference do you hope your products will make in your life?

* What do you hope your business will change in your life?

* Who will benefit from your business besides yourself?

* How will they benefit?

* What has been the highlight of your business so far?

* What is the next goal you are working toward?

* What is your ultimate goal?

If you are setting out on a skin-care, weight-loss, or nutritional program, take photos to document the change. Capture special events on camera to support the story of your business.

We all have a story to tell and we all love listening to stories. Use your experiences and your imagination to create a story that brings your products and your business to life. Your sincerity and enthusiasm will shine through your words.

PART II

Identify Your Best Prospects

Get Ready to Connect!

YOU ARE READY TO START WORKING on the most exciting part of the business—matchmaking! Matchmaking is about finding people who are perfect for your business because your business is perfect for them.

The more people you approach, the more will sign. But it doesn't stop there. Not every recruit will become a producer. If you sign ten people, how many will end up producing little or nothing? These people may not have what it takes or they may have signed up for the wrong reasons. A realistic goal is ending up with three producers based on my experience.

That leaves seven. How many of the seven will end up working the industry average of less than five hours a week? Five is a reasonable estimate.

That leaves two. After six months, will both people become top producers? Probably not. A high percentage of representatives run out of steam after nine months or so because they are unable to make the transition from selling to friends and family to the wider community. At this point, they either leave the business or become minimal producers. Let's say one of our hopefuls leaves within that time frame.

That leaves one lone star a year, from ten new recruits! This means you have to recruit a large number of people to find the superstars who will grow your organization as you help them grow theirs.

Hope is not a business plan. You will set yourself up for disappointment if you expect every new recruit to shine. Some people can talk up a storm, but when it comes to doing anything—they're a washout. Others have heads so filled with dreams that there is no room for the discipline needed to succeed.

The more leads you have, the better your odds of finding the right people—whether they're hot leads, warm leads, or new leads.

Hot Leads

Hot leads include your current list of friends, family, colleagues, customers, neighbors, and the people you interact with regularly—your hairdresser, personal trainer, banker, doctor, delivery person, and dentist. They are hot leads because you already have a relationship, and you can specifically target their circumstances. These are the people to call first.

Warm Leads

To build your business beyond your inner circle, you need to reach new people. Everyone in your inner circle has his or her own inner circle, and you have to find a way to enter it. The more circles you successfully enter, the more warm leads you will generate. Party planners have an advantage in the hostess program, which rewards hostesses for introducing you to their friends.

New Leads

Aim to generate fresh leads all the time to keep your business growing. One new person a day is a minimum if you are serious about building your organization. If you wake every morning knowing you have to find a new contact and keep your antenna up, you will learn how to spot them.

And here is where to start. The millions of representatives who already have a direct selling, network marketing, or party plan business, and the thousands who start one every day provide a wealth of information as to *who* is most likely to be attracted to business, *why* they joined, and *how* to approach them to increase the likelihood of a yes response.

Can you predict who is most likely to start a direct selling business? Absolutely! The information I have gathered over twenty-five years across a wide range of companies paints a very clear picture of prime prospects.

I am about to explain why they are hot prospects and what to do and say to turn them into recruits. I will even show you how to ask questions that will have hot prospects identifying themselves.

Sometimes you will come across prospects so perfect for your business that the "hot prospect alert" will blare loud and clear in your head. The catch is that they are such prime prospects you may not be the only one to recognize their potential. How well you connect on a personal level will determine whether they sign with you or another sponsor.

At other times, you will encounter prospects whose potential is less obvious, or even hidden. Don't be deterred. Just because a prospect is sending out weak signals doesn't make the person a poor prospect. The fact that other less-skilled recruiters may overlook the person's potential makes him or her a great prospect for you.

Of course, every corporation is different, with a unique vision, culture, product range, and plan. However, there are enough common denominators to take the guesswork out of recruiting. You are about to learn these denominators.

As you look for people to connect with, aim for balance. Businesses need leaders and followers, enthusiasts and moderates, cheerleaders and thinkers. Any business that leans heavily on a narrow base is unstable.

Network marketing is no different. Cast your net beyond familiar, easy, or obvious targets. When you broaden the range and the number of people you recruit, your business will be less vulnerable to the performance, behavior, and whims of a few. The more diverse your organization, the more welcoming it will be to a wider demographic.

Recruiting Your Customers

THE FIRST PLACE TO LOOK for recruits is among your existing customers. More than half of all new recruits come through the door marked *customers*. They used and loved the product before they started selling it.

Shoppers are spoilt for choice. Whether they are looking for quality, quantity, or a bargain, there is a product and a price to suit. They're more knowledgeable, more discerning, and less susceptible to spin.

You can safely assume when someone chooses to buy your product that he or she likes it. You can also safely assume the person likes you or he or she wouldn't be buying from you.

The best promotion for any product is word-of-mouth endorsement from people who have used and liked the products. And network marketing is no different—except for one significant detail. Traditional marketers do not pay people who promote their products, but network marketers do. Where better to look for people to sell your products than among the people already using them?

Not all will become movers and shakers, but you need loyal users as much as you need business builders. Industry statistics indicate that seven out of ten representatives will always be small players. Don't let this deter you from signing up your customers. Small players account for a high percentage of sales in most network marketing organizations. Because you are paid on the total sales generated by your organization, it doesn't matter how many representatives contribute to your volume. The more the merrier.

Network marketers fall into five categories:

1. *Home buyers.* They join to purchase products for their own use at wholesale prices. Home buyers are motivated by the discounts they receive for buying directly and the convenience of home delivery. Enhancements such as the auto-shipping of orders direct from the corporation to the customer have dramatically increased the number of home buyers.

2. *Cheerleaders.* As well as buying products for their personal use, cheerleaders service a small circle of close friends and family members. Cheerleaders are motivated by a love of the product and by the opportunity to buy their own products cheaper or to get them free.

3. *Representatives.* These active sellers are motivated by the income they earn selling to a regular base of customers through parties and networking.

4. *Managers.* These star representatives earn regular income and rewards, including cars and vacations for servicing their own customers and for recruiting and training other representatives to do the same.

5. *Business Builders.* The focus of these top income earners is finding and developing managers. Business builders are motivated by the recognition, income, and rewards they enjoy from the large volume of products sold through their downline organization. They are the role models who inspire others to aim high.

Although customers join for different reasons and with different aspirations, what they have in common is a love of your product. This makes every customer a hot prospect.

The following seven steps will turn more of your customers into your recruits:

1. *Service them consistently.* The big payoff for servicing your customers is gaining recruits. Be proactive. Don't wait for your customers to call you. When a product your customer likes comes on special or a new product is launched, contact the person immediately. Be sure to let the customer know he or she was first on your list.

If you have too many customers to call every month, stay in touch by post and e-mail. If your company offers an automated customer newsletter service, subscribe to it. Anything that keeps your name in front of your customers is good value. Spontaneous gestures such as birthday cards and thank-you notes tell your customers they are appreciated. Never underestimate the power of a personal note or a free sample to show you appreciate their business.

The more contact you have with your customers, the easier it will be to decide when to approach them and to tailor your approach to fit their circumstances. Because you have established a relationship, they will be more receptive to your business call when it comes.

2. *Take every opportunity to sow seeds about the business.* Use a well-timed sentence or two in every call. Don't be heavy-handed. You can say a lot in a few seconds. Every seed should address a different aspect of the business, such as the following examples:

"I love helping people buy their products direct and [company name] is such a fun company to work with."

"I was looking for a part-time job and never imagined I would

find a career as rewarding as this. I love the freedom of working when I choose and with whom I choose."
"Working from home means I can deduct my expenses off my income tax."

3. *Keep your antenna up for champions.* Ask your customers for feedback. If they say, "I love the products," you should respond, "I love them too. That why I chose [company name] when I started my business. I can't believe I get paid for recommending products I love using myself."

Keep in mind not everyone likes to shout from the rooftops about their favorite products. Only by inviting feedback from all your customers will you find your cheerleaders and your quiet enthusiasts, and start the process of bringing them into the business. You can afford to take it gently. Your customers' intentions when they start may not indicate their true potential. Industry surveys suggest as many as 90 percent of direct sellers start with small or short-term goals in mind. Customers who intend to be home buyers may blossom into productive sellers or even managers once they have had a taste of the business and the benefit of your inspiring leadership, training, and support.

4. *When you gauge the time is right to make your approach, don't rush in.* Start the call with a simple, "First of all, I want to thank you for being one of my favorite customers," and you will set the right tone.

Continue with a genuine, sincere compliment, such as, "I always look forward to talking with you. You are so enthusiastic/approachable."

Be direct when you explain why you're calling. You might ask, "Have you ever thought about becoming a representative? Of all my customers, you are someone I would really like to work with." Or, "I am always looking for role models/enthusiasts like you." If the answer is yes, you are on your way.

5. *Listen carefully.* If the prospect says, "Yes, but . . . ,'" or, "Not me," you are about to learn valuable information. Listen without interrupting so that you know what the sticking point is.

A response of "I couldn't do that" may signal a lack of confidence. Avoid the temptation to dismiss the prospect's concerns. "Yes you could!" is a poor answer, as it tramples on his or her feelings, and that is not going to win you any points. Asking, "What makes you think that?" shows genuine interest.

A response of "It's not my thing" is an opportunity to turn the conversation to your prospect's past jobs. You might ask the following questions:

"What is the best job you've had?"
"What did you like about it?"
"What was the worst? Why?"
"What's your perfect job?"

6. *Tailor your approach to suit your customer's personality.* For example, if your customer is a bright spark, you may like to try a creative approach.

You might try this approach: "How would you like to come to Maui? The company just launched a promotion and anyone who qualifies gets to go free! A few of us are working toward it and having a live wire like you along would be great."

The objective of the call is to set up an interview, not to sell the business, so don't get so carried away with enthusiasm that you start overselling. If the conversation is going well—stop it. The peak of the conversation is the perfect time to say, "Let's meet for half an hour so we can talk more. This business isn't for everyone, but I have a feeling you would be a great fit. We certainly need people with your credibility/passion. But you'll know in a few minutes if it is for you."

You have complimented your prospects and taken the stress out of the approach by making it clear you are not going to pressure the person. Even if the person declines, he or she will be flattered to have been singled out.

7. *Don't sign your customers up as home buyers and stop contacting them once they start ordering direct.* When your

customer signs, a completely new relationship begins. Once they're on the first step of the ladder, you can take them up step by step.

To turn a customer into a home buyer, you might say, "You are one of my best customers. How would you like to buy your products wholesale?"

To turn a home buyer into a cheerleader, you might say, "Did you know you could earn enough to get your products free, just by servicing a few customers?"

To turn a cheerleader into a representative, let the person know you are impressed by his or her sales. After a few months of consistent orders, you might say, "You are a natural seller," or "Your enthusiasm is contagious. How would you like to earn an extra $500 a month?"

From representative to manager is a short step up the ladder, because the only difference is learning to share enthusiasm and skills with others. You can say, "Let's meet up next week. I want to talk to you about taking your business a step further. You would make a great manager."

You won't have problems turning managers into business builders. Expose them to the benefits enjoyed by the top income earners, and the cream will rise to the top.

CHAPTER NINE

Recruiting at Parties

IF YOU ARE A PARTY PLANNER, there is no better place to find new recruits than at parties. Whether you call them shows, classes, presentations, group consultations, experiences, or demonstrations, parties are a prime location for finding new people. Regardless of how much effort you put into it, you will never have a better opportunity to recruit.

Parties are great recruitment opportunities because the people who go to parties are the same people who host parties and who start their own party plan businesses. Your prospects have already qualified themselves by attending the party. And here is the best part. You'll earn income on your sales while you prospect for new recruits, so you can't lose.

If you are not a party planner, don't skip this chapter. Service clubs, church groups, community organizations, and professional associations all need speakers with an interesting, topical story to tell. You can adapt these ideas to any group situation.

There could be any number of reasons why your guest is at the party, including:

★ She loves going to parties.

★ She is your hostess's best friend.

★ There was nothing on television.

★ She is the victim of emotional blackmail ("I came to *your* party . . .").

★ She is interested in your products.

★ She is already a customer and wants to reorder.

★ She wants a night away from her husband and kids.

★ She couldn't come up with an excuse.

★ She is thinking about hosting her own party.

★ She is looking for a part-time job.

★ She is considering a full-time business.

★ Everyone else in her circle was going.

All you can count on is that there will be as many reasons as there are guests. It doesn't matter why she is there. You have a captive audience and an incredible opportunity to interest people in your business. Every guest is a potential recruit, from your prime prospect the hostess to the accidental prospect who never considered the business until you planted those seeds.

Follow these twelve steps to turn every party into a recruiting fest.

Step One

Approach every party with a prospecting mind-set. From the moment you make the booking, as you coach your hostess, prepare for your party, drive to the house, unload the car, and walk up to the door, focus on your goal: "I will identify three prospects and one of them will become my next recruit."

Step Two

The more guests in the room the better your chance of finding prospects, so do whatever it takes to increase numbers. Use your Host Rewards program to motivate your hostess, help her with the invitation list, and tempt her with extra gifts—do whatever it takes to fill the room.

If numbers are small, encourage your hostess to think of people she may have overlooked.

"Have you invited your son's teacher/boss's wife?"

"What about your children's friends? Perhaps their parents may like to get to know you a little better."

"Is there someone at the golf club/book club/church you especially like?"

Keep your hostess motivated by asking, "Have you chosen the free products you want? I want you to have as much as possible."

Small numbers are better than none, so if your hostess is struggling to get numbers or suggests postponing, say, "Don't worry. I reserved the date for you and it would be hard to book another party at short notice. We'll have fun even if numbers are small. Have you thought about inviting your hairdresser, doctor, or sister-in-law? Has a new neighbor moved into the area? Is there someone at the gym who seems friendly? What about the receptionist?"

Offer last-minute incentives to encourage your hostess to pull out all the stops, by saying:

"If you find two more guests, I will give you [extra gift or a discount voucher]."

"Let guests know I have a gift for anyone who brings a friend."

The number-one reason confirmed guests become no-shows is that they forget to attend. Reduce that risk with an e-mail to guests the night before your party along these lines:

> Hi Grace,
>
> Thank you for coming to Samantha's party. I am looking forward to meeting you. You are about to experience [add a sentence that highlights the best part of the party].
>
> See you on Thursday at 7 P.M. I know your time is valuable, so we will be finished by 8.30 P.M.
>
> Sarah
>
> P.S. Bring a guest who has not already been invited, and I have a special gift for you.

Call guests without an e-mail address, leaving a voice mail message if they do not answer.

Step Three

Prepare to recruit. Take at least three business packs to the party with information on your opportunity and a gift that will increase the eye appeal, such as an inexpensive novelty item (scoot around your local discount store and you'll spot some bargains) or your own products purchased when they were on special. Display the packs in a colorful bag, basket, or gift box and make sure you position them prominently at the party.

Not only will the packs be a powerful visual reminder that your top priority is to identify prospects to give them to, they also will attract the guests' attention.

Step Four

As you set up, ask your hostess which guests she thinks would make great party planners. The more information you have, the better your chances of making a connection. For each name she mentions, you should ask, "What made you choose her?"

Step Five

Start recruiting the moment the first guest walks through the door. As you greet each arrival think, "Is this my next prospect?"

We all like people who like us, so be warm and interested. What you learn will be the basis of the seeds you plant throughout your presentation and cultivate during your one-on-one time at the end of the party. Ask yourself:

"Who will I enjoy working with most?"
"Who looks the most interesting?"
"Who looks the most interested?"
"Who is the friendliest?"
"Who looks like he or she needs to change jobs?"
"Who is pregnant?"

Step Six

After you have thanked your hostess and welcomed guests, play this icebreaker game to identify your hottest prospect—the ultimate partygoer. When you explain the winner will receive one of your eye-catching gift packs, you can guarantee everyone will participate.

The game takes only a few minutes to play, and you can adapt the questions to suit your audience. Make sure all guests have a pen and paper, and invite them to award themselves points as follows:

★ One point for each party you have been to in the last two years.

★ Two points for each party you have been to in the last six months.

★ Three points for each party you have hosted.

★ Five points for parties you hosted in the last six months.

★ Three points if anyone has ever approached you about a direct selling business.

★ Double those points if you seriously considered it.

★ Five points if you have been a representative for any direct selling company.

The guest with the most points wins. When you give the guest the gift pack, be open and enthusiastic about what is in it. Tell the winner, "Congratulations! You have won [this amazing body scrub] and I have popped in some information about our company that I think you will find interesting."

You have identified your first prospect: the social person who loves to attend and host parties. It's a short step from hosting to selling, and you can pursue that track the next day. Two to go.

Step Seven

Make the party a compelling commercial for your business. No one will complain if the commercial is entertaining and informative! You are there to showcase your products, but that is the easy part. Recruiting takes a little more skill.

Pepper your presentation with a variety of minicommercials for your business. Introduce the commercials smoothly into the flow of your product presentation, keeping each one short and to the point.

> **"I love this business because everybody wins. Our customers get great products at great prices, our hostesses get free products for hosting the party, and I get to work with these amazing products."**

"The company backs us all the way. The training is incredible and we all get together once a year at our annual convention. I've never had a job that's so much fun."

"Most of us work part-time; some of us on top of a regular job. But we're finding more people are looking for a complete change of career and want to work the business full-time. Everyone is different, and that is the beauty of being self-employed—you choose the hours that suit you."

Make sure your commercials address different aspects of the business. We all have different hot buttons. The more buttons you push, the greater your chances of connecting with more guests.

* A college student may be eager to earn money over the summer or to pay off a student loan.

* A business complementing an existing business—for example, nutrition products for a health practitioner or skin-care products for an aesthetician—will make sense to an entrepreneur.

* A monthly car allowance will start someone who needs a new car thinking about the advantages of her own business. "Who gets to drive a company car? Who wishes she did?"

* Anyone who loves to travel will be excited by free vacations. "I am working toward a free trip to the Bahamas and my husband gets to come along as well. Does anyone here work for a company that pays for her annual vacation?"

* A part-time job will appeal to someone with cash-flow problems (think holidays, tax time, school fees, or unexpected bills).

"When my son Mason was born we had over $8,000 on our credit card. It was costing us $1,600 a year in interest! I managed to pay off the card doing just two parties a week."

You can cover an endless number of benefits when you keep your commercials short:

> "The best part is being able to spend time with my family, and have time to myself, doing what I love doing."
> "My skin has never looked better."
> "I lost five pounds in the first week."

Support your stories with facts:

> "Everyone receives training in the basics to help them get started, but the training never stops."
> "Please feel free take a look at my training manual." Take your manual to every party to give you a lead-in to the person who is the most interested. "I noticed you looking through my manual . . ."

Don't shy away from talking about money. All workers are paid for their efforts. Instead of earning a salary, you have chosen to be rewarded for your results. People will applaud your initiative and someone in the group may think, "It sounds fabulous—I wonder if I could do what she is doing?"

Step Eight

In the following chapters, you will discover how wide-reaching your prospect base is and the best recipients for your packs. However, a quick and easy way to encourage a hot prospect to identify herself is to ask, "Who tried out for the cheerleading squad?"

Here is a promise. Your cheerleaders will volunteer the information faster than you can say "pom-pom." Think for a minute. Party planning fits the fun-loving, attention-seeking cheerleader personality like a glove. If she's a mom, you can bet she is missing the fun and the thrill. One simple question and a red-hot prospect has just identified herself. You'll have no problem identifying prospects if you stay focused. Don't forget to note which guests receive the business packs, as you explain why you chose them.

> "When Tayla starts school next week, this could be the ideal job for you. I started when my son Brayden went to school so I could pick him up every day."
>
> "This is for you for asking such great questions."
>
> "You look amazing in that outfit. I wish all my customers could see you modeling it."
>
> "You have helped us all have such fun tonight."

Step Nine

Close with an invitation to consider the business, adding specific information about how the business works. "If you've had fun tonight, you should think about doing what I do. All it costs to start is $[. . .] and you are in business! You choose how much you earn. Whether you want to earn a few dollars doing one party a week or work toward a six-figure income is up to you."

Step Ten

Use your one-on-one time to connect with the guests who show the most potential.

"Catherine, have you ever thought about doing this? Of everyone here tonight, you would make the best [consultant/representative/distributor]." You can bet Catherine will ask, "Why do you say that?"

Your sincere response might be:

> "You have a great way with people. Everyone seems to like you."
>
> "You have such fabulous skin."
>
> "You have such an enthusiastic personality."

"You obviously know a lot about health."

"You have always been a successful businessperson."

"I can really see you doing this. You are such fun."

Don't neglect guests who didn't come up on your radar during your presentation.

> "Thanks for coming tonight. It has been great getting to know you. What do you usually do Tuesday nights?"
>
> "I can't wait to hear what you think of our products. May I call you next week?"
>
> "Thanks so much for coming tonight. Samantha told me how busy you are. Where do you work?"

Don't hesitate to approach anyone who qualifies. I cannot begin to tell you how many times a new recruit has said to me, "I've been to lots of parties but no one ever asked me before."

Step Eleven

As you total up the party sales, invite your hostess to join and say, "You did a great job tonight. What interesting/lively friends you have." When she replies, "Thanks," you should ask, "Do you know what the hardest part about tonight was?"

You can guarantee she'll ask, "No, what?"

Tell her, "The part you did. Getting people along is the hardest part and you did a great job. All I did was show up and have a great time meeting a bunch of interesting people." Hand her a pack. "I saved this one for you. Did you know if even half the people who came tonight gave you a party, you would [pay off your starter kit, for example]? Our average sale per party is $[. . .] so you would make around $[. . .] and your sales would count toward that free cruise to the Bahamas I was talking about. Can you imagine it?"

Step Twelve

When you call the people who received the packs, try these phrases guaranteed to impress your prospect openers:

"Hi Grace. Thanks for coming last night. It was great to meet you and I have to tell you, if you hadn't won the pack I would have given you one anyway."

She will almost certainly ask, "Why?" You should respond, "Because . . ." and have a sincere reason ready, such as:

". . . I think you would be fun to work with."

". . . being a teacher gives you instant credibility."

". . . I love your energy/enthusiasm. Who wouldn't want to work with you?"

". . . you did most of my job for me. I think you are a natural."

Follow with, "Have you had a chance to read the information I included in the pack?" to help get the conversation flowing.

The objective of the call is to get the interview, not to sell the business, so keep it light and offer your prospect an escape route so she doesn't feel pressured. You might say, "I would love to meet you for half an hour so I can tell you more about it. It's your call, but you'll never know if you don't hear me out. It would be great to see you again, regardless of what you decide."

If you keep it light, compliment your prospects, and make it clear you are not going to pressure them, they will be flattered you approached them, even if they decline.

CHAPTER TEN

Approaching People Who Need the Money

THERE IS A DARK CLOUD over the American dream, and it is getting darker. The gap between what most people have in life and what they need is widening, and that makes almost everybody a hot prospect. The U.S. Census Bureau publishes alarming figures of homeowners defaulting on their mortgage payments. Forty-seven million Americans have no health insurance and eighteen thousand die every year because of it.

Americans without a college education are struggling to adjust to lower wages, harsher working conditions, and reduced benefits.

Retirement is a bleak outlook for many Americans. Far too many retirees will depend on Social Security as their only source of income, which will deny them a decent standard of living.

Even people saving for retirement could be in for a harsh reality check. Half a million dollars invested at 5 percent yields only $25,000 a year—before tax! At best, that will fund only a modest lifestyle. A million dollars on top of a mortgage-free house is closer to the mark when you factor in escalating living expenses.

Need isn't the only angle to consider. Greed is another. Materialism is rampant in our society. Marketers tempt us with an endless flow of new styles and designs, and we fall for it hook, line, and sinker. No sooner do we buy the latest gadget than a better model catches our eye. We pay off our home, only to start dreaming of a vacation home. We return from the trip of a lifetime and an enticing travel offer in the mailbox starts us dreaming again.

Even people who appear wealthy may need money more than appearances suggest. The impressive house, late-model car, and golf club membership may be stressing someone who has run up considerable debt to acquire them. Millions of Americans are living in a fool's paradise and are about to find out how much easier it is to get into debt than out of it.

The dark cloud has a silver lining! It's your business opportunity. Most people could dramatically change their financial situations with a small home-based business to supplement their household income.

How do you find and approach prospects who need money?

You expose their poverty gap. No one is going to buy an aspirin unless he has a headache. If you can get your prospects thinking about what they don't have, or what they could have with a few more dollars in their wallets, you have a good chance of recruiting them.

Our fear of loss is greater than our desire for gain. Fears of never owning their own home, not having enough to live on when they retire, even having less than their friends and neighbors, can all prompt people to think seriously about a business.

The number-one reason people start a business is extra income. If you want them signing with you, find out what is missing in their lives and offer a way to provide it.

Your message has power. Ask, "Why max out your credit cards or use your home as an ATM when a part-time business could provide what you want, debt-free?"

Network marketing is the perfect vehicle to earn funds for

college or retirement, pay for expensive indulgences, or reduce debt. Most bankruptcies could be avoided with an extra $50 a week. Starting a network marketing or party plan business, even if it is only to service a few friends and family members, could save your prospect from hitting rock bottom.

Swamping your prospects with predictions of financial meltdown is not the answer. Let your prospects discover for themselves they need more money, by asking the right questions.

"How much difference would an extra $50 a week make to your life?"

"How much difference would an extra $500 a month make to your life?"

"Does your job pay enough for you to live the life you want?"

"If you had $10,000 to spend, what would you buy?"

"What's your ideal annual income?"

"What difference would that income make to your life?"

"What do you want to do when you retire?"

"How much do you need to maintain your current lifestyle when you retire?"

Of course, you are not going to ask all the questions. Asking a twenty-year-old to think about retirement is as smart as asking a sixty-year-old if he yearns for an iPhone. The more skilled you are at asking questions that match your prospects' current priorities, the better your chances of exposing their "poverty gap," or the difference between what they have and what they want in their lives.

You will increase your chance of your new recruit performing if you focus on prospects with the desire and the drive to succeed.

If you line all 300 million Americans in a row, with the richest at one end and the poorest at the other, here is what you will find:

* ✶ Approximately 5 percent are wealthy. We'll call them Group One.

* ✶ Approximately 20 percent are reasonably well off. We'll call them Group Two.

* ✶ Approximately 50 percent are average earners. We'll call them Group Three.

* ✶ Approximately 20 percent are struggling. We'll call them Group Four.

* ✶ Approximately 5 percent are poor. We'll call them Group Five.

Which are your best prospects?

Not Group One. Even if they want more money, they have almost infinite ways to get it.

Group Two? Possibly. They may have ambitions to move into the highest echelon of income earners. However, industry statistics suggest few of our producers start from that group (although many enter Groups One and Two through their network marketing or party plan business).

Group Three? Absolutely. The real income of the average hardworking American is slipping. They are working harder, but the rising cost of living is keeping them from reaching financial security.

They'll be interested in how to supplement their incomes and how to take advantage of the tax breaks that come with running a home-based business. This group is upwardly mobile, and you have the perfect vehicle for them to get where they want to be.

What about Group Four? These low-average earners are struggling to make ends meet. They share many characteristics with those in Group Three, but they may lack the education or skills to get a better job. Some have been dragged into debt due to misjudgments or misfortune. Healthcare costs are the leading cause of bankruptcy.

These low-paid workers deserve a chance to live a better life, and you have a way to help them achieve it. Regardless of prior education, skills, and experiences, anyone with the courage, determination, and drive to succeed can build a profitable business.

Few network marketers come from the 5 percent of income earners in Group Five. When you prospect based on income needs, set your sights on the 70 percent of the population who fall into the middle and lower-middle range of income earners.

CHAPTER ELEVEN

Turning Parents On to Your Business Opportunity

IF THERE IS A MATCH MADE IN HEAVEN, it is parenting and network marketing.

Children may be priceless, but they also are expensive. From diapers, food, and clothing to education, sports, and vacations, there is no cheap way to raise a family. The U.S. Census Bureau reports it costs between $140,000 and $300,000 to raise a child to the age of eighteen, with an average price tag of $200,000. And that is before college fees, weddings, and coming-of-age celebrations kick in.

The majority of households are two-income families because few single incomes stretch far enough to provide for a family. But working when their children are young puts many parents in an emotional tug-of-war.

Too many think their choices are narrow—either go to work or be a stay-at-home mom. It doesn't have to be that way. "Mompreneurs" can blend both roles. Network marketing is an ideal way to supplement the family income when it is not feasible for

67

both parents to work outside the home. Here are reasons that attract parents to the business.

Family First

Children thrive with their parents at home. The first years shape the rest of a child's life. School-age children who come home each day to a mom or dad are happier and more secure. It is also important to be around when children hit the challenging teen years.

Believe me when I say it's impossible to leave children in day care while you work outside the home and not feel guilty. There are no second chances when it comes to parenting. The precious years when children are young can never be relived.

The Pew Research Center reports only 28 percent of working moms surveyed think they are doing a good job of parenting. Although 60 percent said a part-time job would suit them best, only 24 percent actually have part-time jobs. The last census showed 70 percent of women with children under the age of fifteen worked outside the home. Is that opportunity I hear knocking?

You have a lot to offer parents. Outside of network marketing, few jobs offer the flexibility that allows parents to juggle work and family. Employers who accommodate their workers' family schedules are rare. Most jobs with flexible hours fall into the minimum- or low-wage category.

Network marketing parents can give children their full attention without sacrificing extra income. Mompreneurs can schedule time for family activities *before* their business and can always reschedule when the need arises. "Family first" is the creed of a network marketing or party plan business.

Earning What You Deserve

The reality is that "work" doesn't work for most mothers. Becoming a mother means taking a lifetime pay cut. Surveys reveal taking as few as three years off from work will be penalized by a 37 percent reduction in income.

Not only is the workplace prejudiced against anyone who takes a break from work to raise kids, but it can be harder to find work. A recent investigation revealed résumés hinting at motherhood, such as being active in the Parent Teachers Association, cut the chance of getting the job by 44 percent.

It's not just about mothers. It's dawning on many absentee fathers that their children are growing up without them. The daily commute on top of long working hours means some fathers see their children only on weekends.

Network marketing is different in every way. It does not intrude on family time, costs almost nothing to start, and is self-funding as it grows. Network marketers don't have to pay exorbitant daycare costs, so the money stays where it is earned.

Once you have built an organization of productive people, you continue to earn even when you're not actively working. You could be watching your daughter star in her school play or cheering from the sidelines when your son scores a goal, while your downline distributors are out working.

A Confidence Boost

As rewarding as parenting is, it demands a dramatic change of lifestyle. Your most-read book becomes *The Very Hungry Caterpillar*, and you are pushed to find a skirt without tiny greasy fingerprints on it.

Giving up activities you used to enjoy can lead to a drop in self-esteem. A network marketing business can help parents regain what may be missing in their lives—the chance to make new friends, master new skills, and for some housebound moms, the opportunity and income to dress up once in a while!

Parents who work from home are great role models. Who doesn't want her kids to learn independence and self-reliance? Children who experience how a business works from the inside will have a head start when they start their own businesses.

Life After Kids

The U.S. Census Bureau claims that most of us can expect live till we're seventy-eight years old, so many parents will have half their lives ahead of them once their children turn eighteen. That's a long time to play tennis, golf, or bingo.

Network marketing accommodates all ages and backgrounds. You can start small when the kids are young and fire up the business up when they leave for college.

A good friend once told me, "There are two gifts you can give your kids. The first is a good education and the second is to ensure they're not worrying about you when they leave home."

Empty nesters with few outside interests may place unrealistic expectations on their kids at a time they are preoccupied with raising their own families. Do we want our kids to visit because they want to—or because they feel they should? Parents with adult children could discover a whole new world when they start their network marketing business.

No two parents will have the same priorities. For some, it may be as simple as paying for a college education. For others, it will be the high price they're paying for allowing their children to grow up while they are tied to the office. You will come across parents who don't need the money but are looking for a social outlet or the stimulation of a fresh challenge.

The secret to turning parents on to your opportunity is to push all the buttons and see which ones are hot.

Network marketing is discrimination-free. Whatever their family circumstances, parents will find their niche. The whole family can make a contribution and everyone can share in the rewards.

Parents are joining the business in droves. Capitalize on the trend by positioning your opportunity as the ultimate family business.

CHAPTER TWELVE

Identifying Hot Prospects by Their Careers

MANY OF YOUR PROSPECTS already have careers. Those careers not only are excellent pointers to great prospects, but also will tell you how to approach them.

Prospects whose existing careers match the training and skills needed in network marketing or a party plan business have a higher-than-average chance of succeeding. All they have to do is apply the skills they have already learned in their other jobs. No retraining needed!

The following jobs are already overwhelmingly represented in this industry, so make them the first place you look for prospects.

Teachers

The fact that teachers are highly represented in the industry comes as no surprise. Teachers are organizers and self-starters. They know how to set goals and plan a strategy to produce the outcome they want. Teachers are comfortable in front of an audience, and it's where they like to be. Their above-average communication skills make them persuasive marketers.

What would switch a teacher to your opportunity? Teaching is highly demanding. There is increasing pressure on teachers' time. Many have to cope with crowded classrooms, students needing help with basic skills, and behavioral problems. Health and safety compliance issues are adding more to their workload.

Many teachers chose teaching for the flexible hours and vacations that suited them and their families. Network marketing offers even more flexibility.

Ask teachers if they think they're overworked, undervalued, and underpaid and you will get a resounding "Yes!" No wonder they look for a life after the classroom and find it in our industry.

Artists

Artists aren't typically thought of as great businesspeople, but this is an unfortunate stereotype. Creative people are attracted to and embrace the creativity of the business. They think outside the box, and they love to express themselves. There's more than a little showmanship in being a party planner or network marketer, and this is an area at which artists excel.

You can count on a willing ear when you approach artists, because they probably need the money, and they certainly need flexibility so they can pursue their creative talents. Artists are passionate about what they do, and they love the recognition that goes with success.

Take a broad-brush approach to finding artistic prospects. Think painters, craftspeople, singers, landscapers, performers, sculptors, florists, chefs, dancers, actors, writers, poets, photographers, scrapbookers, and musicians. Anyone whose full-time job or part-time interest is creative expression will bask in the entrepreneurial, encouraging, and supportive environment of network marketing.

Nurses

Nurses are drawn to network marketing for good reason. Anyone who represents the caring profession is nurturing, supportive, and hardworking. Their genuine desire to help others indicates a perfect fit for this business.

Nurses are under incredible pressure—a healthcare system in chaos is not a healthy environment to work in. Erratic hours, chronic staff shortages, the risk of contagious diseases, and increasing demands on their time can easily lead to stress, exhaustion, and burnout.

Network marketing is an opportunity to make a worthwhile contribution without sacrificing your own sanity. Their natural empathy helps nurses build strong relationships, and their genuine desire to help others makes them nurturing leaders.

Engineers

Engineers have the best of both worlds when it comes to network marketing. They are both creative and disciplined.

Visionary engineers are quick to spot the potential of the business, and their focus and discipline makes them natural business builders. Network marketing offers them more scope for social activities and more recognition for their talents. No wonder engineers are attracted to and prosper in network marketing.

Salespeople

People in sales will be ripe for your approach. Their charismatic, persuasive personalities are a great fit and they are motivated by the reward-for-results nature of the business.

Naturally competitive and motivated, salespeople love the recognition that comes with success. Their enthusiasm, energy, and drive will rub off on the people they work with.

Why network marketing? Car, realty, insurance, and other sales professionals' average earnings don't come close to matching your high-income, high-reward opportunity. Don't be afraid to openly compare compensation plans and earnings, not just for the average performer but also the highest achievers.

Health Professionals

Across the board—from doctors, dentists, chiropractors, psychologists, and therapists to dermatologists, naturopaths, homeopaths, and physiotherapists—health professionals have the credibility and the confidence to build successful network marketing businesses.

The most glaring shortcoming of healthcare jobs is time. Income is pegged to the number of hours worked or appointments held. When the last patient walks out the door each day, the income stops. Another shortcoming is the rising cost of liability insurance, which is cutting deeply into the profits of health professionals.

Network marketing is different on all counts. It costs little to start and run, and there is no major liability insurance required. Although it takes time and dedication to build a business, the rewards continue to flow through the residual income you earn from your downline organization.

Health professionals enjoy high levels of respect and admiration. That credibility carries over into their network marketing business. They can blend both careers. Nutritional and even skincare products can complement an existing health business, especially as the focus moves toward preventive health management.

Support Professionals

Career counselors, service professionals, and human resource managers feature high on the list of professions represented.

Their training gives them a head start when it comes to understanding and mentoring their recruits. They are hardworking. They have advanced interpersonal training and skills. What better qualities could you have to start your own business?

Now that you know which jobs indicate skills that suggest a perfect fit for direct selling and the circumstances that indicate a change may be on the cards, how do you approach people based on their jobs? Try these ideas for starters:

★ Keep your antenna up for people who work in jobs that best fit your opportunity. Make it a habit to ask everyone you meet, "What do you do?" Asking someone about his or her job is an easy conversation starter.

If the person responds, "Nurse [or artist, or . . .]," say, "That's interesting. [Nurses] do very well in my business." You can almost guarantee the response will be, "What do you do?" and you can take it from there.

★ If you are a party planner, ask every guest at every party to say what he or she does. Find a match and consider that guest a prospect. Either hand the person one of your business packs or say, "You're a realtor? I have something to talk to you about later." At the very least, the person will be intrigued to hear you out when you call and say, "I'm very interested in your take on my business."

★ Scroll through your contacts list looking for people who work in one of the promising jobs. Call and say, "I just discovered something that may interest you. Did you know we have more teachers in my business than most other professions?" You can bet the response will be, "Why is that?" and you have your invitation to explain.

★ You have a dream opener if you and your prospects have or had the same job. You already talk the same language and the person will be interested in your reasons for switching or for choosing to supplement your career with a network marketing business. You can say, "I used to be [your past job] before I started my business—now I earn as much in two hours as I used to earn in two days. Plus, I hated the office politics. Everyone is so supportive and friendly here."

✷   Consider running an opportunity event or business seminar that targets a specific group of professionals. Make sure your speakers come from careers respected by your target audience. We relate to people who share our background, and there is no better testimony than from someone who has walked in our shoes.

✷   Make it easy to test the waters. Your prospects don't have to give up their regular jobs if they are interested. Teachers can start a business during their summer vacation. Health professionals can test the products' appeal to existing patients. Most people can find a spare hour a day if the motivation is high enough. If it goes well, there may come a time they decide to switch jobs and work the business full-time. And there's your next superstar!

CHAPTER THIRTEEN

Connecting with People Who Have Been in the Business Before

HERE IS SOME GOOD NEWS. Every single day twenty-five thousand new representatives start a direct selling business in the United States, and approximately eighty thousand sign up worldwide. Such an impressive number will give you a huge confidence boost when you are prospecting.

The news gets better. Half of these new recruits will leave the business in the first three months.

And the news gets even better: Four out of five will be gone by the end of the first year.

How is this good news? It's good news because it shows there is a vast reservoir of people who were excited enough in the business to give it a try.

There could be any number of reasons why it didn't work for them the first time, or even second time around:

*   They didn't have clear goals.

*   They weren't motivated enough to give it their best shot.

* The company they chose wasn't right.
* They couldn't summon enough enthusiasm for the products.
* The training didn't meet their needs.
* The timing was wrong.
* They didn't survive the transition from selling to family and friends to selling to the outside world.
* Their sponsors didn't give them the support they needed.
* They moved to a new town.
* They were overcommitted or too many distractions got in the way.
* They got ill, or pregnant, or preoccupied with a new baby.

Perhaps, much like 90 percent of the people who start a direct selling business, they joined with a short-term goal and drifted away once they had achieved it.

The point is that it doesn't matter why they left. What matters is they joined in the first place. Most people do not investigate a range of companies before they sign. Many sign impulsively, with little thought as to whether the company or the products are right for them.

It is easy to get it wrong the first time—choosing the wrong company or failing to get the business off the ground.

The good news for you is the mistake cost them nothing. The value of the products and support new representatives receive far outweighs the cost of the starter kit. There is no reason why your prospects will have bad feelings about the business, and no reason they should not try again, with a different company, a different product range, and a different sponsor—you.

Circumstances change, and they can change dramatically. A spouse may lose a job, a car may need replacing, or the house may need remodeling.

Some people reach a point when their priorities change. More and more road warriors are questioning the toll that traveling takes on their health and personal lives.

Now consider how many were approached, but declined. Ten times the number of those who start is a realistic estimate.

How many of the "no's" were 100 percent convinced the business wasn't for them? Many factors may have influenced their decision—the credibility, likeability, or skill of the person who approached them; the appeal of the products they represented; and their personal circumstances at the time they were approached.

"No" may have meant, "Not with you," "Not with your company," "Not now," or "Not enough information."

The decision will not have been black or white, but somewhere in the vast realm of gray.

Nothing stays the same. That was then, this is now! Everyone who has been in the business before, or even considered it, is ripe for re-signing. These five steps will help you bring them into your organization:

1. Ask every person you meet if he or she has ever been in direct selling or has known anyone in the business. If a person was interested enough to sign up once, your support and experience could make all the difference this time around. Everyone deserves a second chance, so don't hesitate to offer someone another shot at owning his or her own business.

Be prepared to prompt a little. People may be reluctant to tell you about their previous brush with direct selling if they feel they failed. Make it easy for them. Ask direct questions.

"Have you ever been in direct selling?"
"Have you ever been approached?"
"Do you buy any of your products from a direct seller?"

2. Make sure you show empathy with your prospect by saying, "Many people try different companies before they find the right fit."

3. Find out when they joined, what they liked about the business, and what they didn't like. Ask how long they stayed and why they left. Once you break the ice, you will find most people are more than willing to share their experiences. Don't be nervous about hearing something you don't like. Turnover is a fact of life in most jobs. A typical McDonald's unit has a 100 percent staff turnover every year.

4. If you are in the business for the second time around, say so. Share your experiences and explain why it is different for you this time.

> "I know how you feel. I only lasted three months with the first company I joined."
> "I am so happy I heard about this company. It just felt right."

Share your enthusiasm for your current business.

> "The training is incredible."
> "The products practically sell themselves."

Be specific about what is different.

> "I loved selling but I hated doing the deliveries. This company ships all orders direct to my customers so all I have to do is sell."
> "I get so much more support."
> "This company pays for the hostess rewards, so I keep more of my earnings."
> "The plan is so much simpler."
> "I used to feel guilty because I never found enough time to service my customers. This company helps me by sending a monthly newsletter direct to my customers, with my name on it."

5. If you are calling someone who has been referred to you, try this approach:

"I met your sister Kori at a computer class, and she mentioned
you used to be in direct selling. I'm in the business, too!"

A word of caution—don't be so eager to recruit that you
ignore red flags that pop up. If your prospect has genuine concerns about a previous company or sponsor, listen for clues as to
how you can do better, but resist the temptation to agree. Critic-
izing a competitor is a cheap shot, especially as you are hearing
only one side of the story.

Someone who has been with several companies also may not
be a good prospect. You don't want to sign a Debbie Downer
who will poison others in your organization. The previous company may have been delighted to see the back of her.

★ ★ ★ ★ ★

Failure is not a chronic condition. Millions of people in the
business are in it for the second or third time. Many are succeeding spectacularly. They have learned from past mistakes and are
better equipped to succeed this time around.

Not everyone is right for this business, and there are many
valid reasons why some people leave it. However, the vast majority left because of problems that can be overcome by a change of
product, company, or sponsor.

They are prime prospects, they are flooding back into the
recruiting pond every single day, and they are yours for the
asking.

CHAPTER FOURTEEN

Embracing Ethnic Diversity

WHEN MY HUSBAND, WAYNE, and I first arrived in the United States, we traveled around every state to experience our new country firsthand. It took three years, and apart from the awe-inspiring landscape, the rich culture, and the wonderful people we met, our adventure was more fun and more exciting than we had ever imagined.

As Americans in training, our first challenge was learning the language. Emigrating from New Zealand, an English-speaking country, we hadn't expected so many words and phrases to be different or to carry different meanings. More than a few times we would be chatting happily with someone before realizing they didn't have a clue what we were talking about. Friends now kindly tell us if we say something odd or "un-American."

Surprised? Even the Harry Potter series of books written by English author J. K. Rowling have been translated into American—including the titles. Every country, and every ethnic group within that country, incorporates aspects of its culture and develops a unique dialect. It's part of the magic of diversity.

Your business, and your life, will be enriched if you move beyond your comfort zone to embrace diversity. There is a huge talent pool in the 100 million Americans who are Hispanic, African American, or Asian.

Ethnic minorities will play major roles in the growth of this industry, not least because their numbers are growing faster than the general population.

The Asian population is growing at a rate of 3 percent and African Americans at 2 percent. Half of all babies born every year are Hispanic, making it the fastest-growing minority group in America. At 44.5 million, one in seven Americans is Hispanic.

Here is where it gets really interesting. Although the median age of all Americans is 36.2, for non-Hispanic Whites the median age is 40.3, Asian Americans 33.2, African Americans 30, and Hispanics 27.2 years.

These young people are our future. If you want to build a diverse organization, incorporate the following steps into your prospecting strategy:

⋆ Widen your circle of friends and acquaintances. The fastest way to build your business will always be through people you know. Breaking into any group without personal connections will be a tough road. Actively seeking out friendships from a variety of backgrounds will open up a whole world of possibilities for you.

⋆ Try to learn as much as you can about cultures that are different from yours. It's not only insensitive to ignore the core values of people whom we hope to work with, it's a recipe for failure.

⋆ If you do not live in an area that represents a broad spectrum of society, venture out to broaden your circle of contacts. Here are a few places to start:

⋆ Restaurants and shops that cater to specific ethnic groups

⋆ Malls in areas where there are large concentrations of minorities

⋆ Community centers, gyms, and clubs catering to specific ethnicities

⋆ Parades, exhibitions, and festivals marking traditional ethnic celebrations

⋆ Ethnic-specific newspapers and magazines

⋆ Professional associations run by ethnic groups

⋆ Adult education programs such as "English as a second language" classes

⋆ Sports and youth programs in ethnic neighborhoods

Look for specific reasons why your business will appeal. For example, less than 2 percent of management jobs in Fortune 500 corporations are held by Hispanic, African, or Asian women. Encourage anyone whose education and skills holler "management" to question the wisdom of working in an environment where the odds are stacked against her. Show her how investing her skills in starting her own business offers much better odds.

⋆ Respect cultural differences. For example, if you want to involve Asians in your business, be aware that food is ingrained in every aspect of their lives. Show your hospitality by serving food before getting down to business. Always acknowledge older before younger people. Accept the respect Asians show for the head of the household, and don't be surprised when they say they wish to discuss your proposal with a parent or spouse before they commit.

⋆ Demonstrate a genuine desire to connect. For example, if your prospect primarily speaks Spanish, take the time to learn a few words before you approach the person.

⋆ If English is your prospect's second language, make it easy for the person to follow you by doing the following:

- ★ Speak slowly and clearly.

- ★ Use basic words and simple sentences.

- ★ Avoid jargon, slang, or industryspeak.

- ★ Pause often to give the prospect time to absorb what you are saying.

- ★ Watch for signs the person understands you, such as maintaining eye contact, nodding, smiling, or asking questions.

If your prospects aren't receiving what you're transmitting, you are wasting your time and theirs.

★ Make sure your products, training materials, and support programs meet your prospects' needs. For example, ensure that your cosmetics are suitable for darker skin tones and that your company literature features African American models before you approach African Americans.

★ If you are not sure about the correct protocols to follow, ask! Trying to do the right thing will be appreciated by any prospect.

It will take time and effort to reach out to prospects from all ethnic groups, but the rewards will be worth it. Not only will you dramatically increase the pool of talent you have to draw from, you and your business will benefit from the perspective and contribution of a diverse range of recruits.

CHAPTER FIFTEEN

Helping Business Owners Switch

FIFTEEN PERCENT OF AMERICANS are self-employed, and according to the U.S. Census Bureau, the number of Americans working from home is growing at twice the rate of the U.S. workforce.

Privately owned businesses are the backbone of the U.S. economy. Small businesses account for half the country's total output and employ half the private-sector workforce. Half of all small businesses are home-based.

The spirit of entrepreneurialism is alive and kicking. Look at the number of day care centers, niche retailers, florists, cafés, spas, nail and hair salons, gyms, home services, and business support centers in your town.

Many of these entrepreneurs are shackled by long lease agreements, increasing compliance costs, hefty loan payments, and staffing woes. Long hours working for little reward is the norm. Often the profits go straight into the coffers of lenders and landlords. Few business owners have a funded retirement plan or health insurance.

Less than half of all private businesses survive to celebrate their fourth anniversary, according to the American Small Business Administration. That adds up to a lot of broken dreams.

It doesn't have to be that way. A network marketing or party plan business is an opportunity to own your business without taking on the burden of going it alone. It costs almost nothing to start and very little to run. There is no upfront capital investment required, apart from a small outlay for a starter kit, so you can own your own business without capital behind you or having to borrow to get started. There is no ceiling on what you can earn, and you don't have to sacrifice family and friends to join the highest echelon of achievers.

How do you position your opportunity to an existing business owner or someone looking for one?

The numbers are already on your side. Fifteen million entrepreneurs currently have a network marketing or party plan business and the momentum is building.

Here are the messages you need to share:

* Bricks and mortar do not make a business. People make a business. If your prospect needs the reassurance of a building, forward him or her photos of the corporate home office.
* If your prospect has big dreams of financial freedom, quote Warren Buffet, who called direct selling "an investor's dream."
* Drop a few names to impress your prospect. Warren Buffett, one of the richest men in the world, and *Virgin* entrepreneur Richard Branson both own network marketing companies.

As great as it is to have the confidence of these credible figures, your best recruiting tools are your own experiences. How could any business owner fail to recognize the synergy in a partnership where one party takes care of the back end of the business and the other concentrates on the front-end activities that produce income?

Imagine! No business plan, no inventory, no bank loan, no premises, no landlord, no staff, and no pressure. If it doesn't work out, your prospect can walk away having risked nothing and lost nothing. A network marketing business offers all the benefits of being self-employed and none of the fear factors.

Another avenue to explore is the interest people have in investing in a business model that to me defies belief—franchising! Why would anyone invest in a costly franchise when network marketing offers a better business model? Franchisees typically pay start-up costs of $100,000 and higher, annual franchise fees averaging $25,000, and ongoing royalties and marketing contributions that wipe out around 10 percent of revenue. If that is not scary enough to put anyone off buying a franchise, consider this—the franchise industry is largely unregulated!

Quite frankly, your business is better and if you don't market it, no one is going to know. The more widely you promote your opportunity, the greater your chance of attracting the attention of someone who currently owns, is thinking about, or actively investigating a business.

Network marketing is a no-risk opportunity to own a business that has low ongoing overhead and high returns from day one! Strict regulations protect both you and your customers.

Apart from a small outlay for the starter kit, your corporate partner invests in you. If it doesn't work out, you don't have to untangle yourself from a contract. You can walk away anytime you want, and for any reason, having lost nothing.

There are millions of people out there who don't know about, or don't understand, our industry. Think of it as a people's franchise. We offer all the benefits of a franchise—the products, the marketing, the expertise, and the support—with none of the costs or restrictions.

Every business owner is a prospect. Long hours, low returns, late payers, and clients who default on their bills foil too many entrepreneurs' dreams. Seek them out, and invite them to switch to your incredible low-risk, high-reward business opportunity.

CHAPTER SIXTEEN

Peacocks and Other Hot Prospects

EVERY BUSINESS LEADER KNOWS that the smartest way to build a great team is to hire personality and train skills. That is because you can't create great personalities, but you can teach the skills needed to get the job done.

If personality didn't matter, employers would hire staff from their résumés alone. But they don't. An impressive résumé only gets you the interview. The interview—where the employer gets to evaluate the real you—gets you the job!

Network marketing is no different. Every single skill needed to succeed can be learned on the job. Finding the right personalities to build your organization is what counts.

We all like to think of ourselves as unique, a one-of-a-kind model. And we are. There are as many different personalities as there are people on this planet. It is also true we share characteristics with other people. These shared personality traits enable us to be grouped into personality types.

Although my goal is not to turn you into an amateur psychologist, you'll create more opportunities to build your organization if you learn to recognize and respond to different personalities. Not only will it help you identify prospects, but you'll know how to approach them and how to mentor them when they join.

Clues to our personalities are written in the way we walk, talk, and listen. More clues come from where we live, how we furnish our homes, and the cars we drive. We send out signals with the clothes we wear and the jobs we do. We reveal a lot through whom we choose as friends and the relationship we have with them. Clues to our personalities can be found in what we read, the programs we watch on television, and how we spend our leisure time. Every single aspect of our lives, even how we respond to pressure, reveals our true personality.

Perhaps recruiting superstars do have a secret after all. They develop the art of reading people and communicating from their perspective. They know the fastest way to create empathy and trust is to identify and adapt to their prospects' personalities.

When you step into the other person's shoes it will be easier to start relationships. You will know which buttons to push to excite people about your opportunity. So, how do you learn to read other people's personalities?

To help you develop your people skills in a way that is simple to learn, fun to practice, easy to remember, and easy to use when training recruits, I have linked each personality to a well-known bird.

Start by making a list of people you are closest to, as it will be easier to analyze people you know:

* Yourself
* Your partner
* Your children
* Your siblings
* Your friends
* Your current team members
* Bosses and coworkers

- ✶ People you admire
- ✶ Someone you don't have a great relationship with
- ✶ Someone who intrigues you, or someone you can't quite work out

Have fun matching the people on your list to one of the birds described next. All you have to do is fit their personal characteristics to the birds they most resemble. You don't have to do this solo. Invite friends, family, and team members to analyze themselves and others. You can do this around a dinner table, in the work cafeteria, or at a training meeting.

Once you feel you have mastered the technique, apply it to every person you meet. Your prospect base will expand dramatically when you reach out to a broader spectrum of people. If you teach your new recruits to master the art of personality-based prospecting, the potential is limitless.

Comparing personalities to birds will also help you to become a more empathetic communicator. When you appreciate their perspective, you will find it easier to make people feel good about themselves—and you! What better foundation can there be for a strong relationship?

Peacocks

Peacocks are driven by attention. They love the limelight.

Peacocks are larger than life. They are colorful, spontaneous, and passionate. They radiate warmth and they make friends easily. Peacocks love socializing, especially when they are the center of attention. They are enthusiastic and extroverted, and they love to talk. We count on them to let us know about the latest movie, restaurant, or celebrity gossip. We invite them to our parties to dazzle us with their sparkling wit and bubbly personalities.

You are a peacock if you are fun to be around, even if you often grab more than your share of the conversation. You are a peacock if you talk fast and often. You are a peacock if you pick up the phone as soon as you find yourself alone and if you can't imagine life without your cell phone. You are a peacock if you have been known to exaggerate or embellish a story for effect. You are a peacock if you love clothes and can't wait to try the latest fashions.

Peacocks are interested in others but they can be fickle if their attention is distracted by something new. There is never a dull moment around peacocks, although they can be exhausting company. Extreme peacocks will do anything to get attention.

How Peacocks Fit the Business

Peacocks are natural networkers. Their vitality and spontaneity are ideal for this business. Their enthusiasm is infectious and their magnetic personalities easily attract customers and recruits. They tend to be undisciplined when it comes to mundane tasks such as record keeping, and they sometimes leave a trail of unfinished projects behind them as they switch from task to task. They have difficulty remembering dates and details and can be unreliable at times. But they brighten every room they enter and we soon forgive them their forgetfulness.

How to Approach Peacocks

Sell the sizzle and stay way from detail, or you risk losing your peacock's attention. They are easily distracted. Let them do most of the talking. Peacocks will not be interested in the finer points of the compensation plan, but they will be excited by the trips, rewards, and conventions—especially the chance to glam up at the awards banquet. Peacocks are impulsive, so don't be surprised if they decide to join on the spot.

How to Keep Peacocks Motivated

Peacocks will work hard for recognition and rewards. Dangle lots of carrots in front of peacocks to keep them focused.

Encourage peacocks to take advantage of every automated or time-saving tool the company offers, so they can spend their time at the front line where they are the most effective. Let them bask in the glow of frequent praise and keep them working by reminding them they may get to take the stage on awards night. Stay in contact by phone and in person. Chances are they will forget to open their e-mail or respond to your voice-mail message.

High-maintenance peacocks have short attention spans and are easily bored. They need constant stimulation to stay motivated but with the right leadership will deliver outstanding results. They love to mentor others, especially when they are publicly acknowledged by their protégés.

Doves

Doves are driven by the desire to make a worthwhile contribution. They want to be valued.

Doves are sensitive, nurturing, and kind. True friends, they will go out of their way to help others. You can count on doves to be there when you need them. They may appear reserved until they know you, but they will stay loyal once the friendship is established. Doves are drawn to jobs where they can help others in a meaningful way.

You are a dove if you're a good listener or if people ask for your help and confide in you. You are a dove if you avoid conflict and try to be a peacemaker. You are a dove if you prefer to keep your opinions to yourself, but you are tolerant of different perspectives and viewpoints. You would rather turn away from a disagreement than hurt someone's feelings. You are a dove if you enjoy giving and receiving gifts, you remember birthdays, and you ask what you can bring if you are invited for a meal.

The dove's empathy, generosity, and selflessness earn them the affection and respect they deserve, but their kind natures make them vulnerable to being taken advantage of. Although they may resent it, they have difficulty saying no, so they often end up taking on more than their share of commitments. Extreme doves sacrifice their own goals to serve others.

How Doves Fit the Business

Doves truly care about others and enjoy helping them reach their potential. Doves are attentive to their customers, although they have to overcome their reluctance to approach people about their business. Supportive and intuitive, they make great mentors once they learn to stop mothering and start managing their people.

Doves take their responsibilities seriously and are proud when their protégés earn praise and recognition. They do not seek public acclaim but like to know their support is appreciated.

How to Approach Doves

Make sure you don't overlook a dove because she is not putting herself forward. Doves can be quiet, especially when they are in large groups. Approach them first, but don't push. Doves are conservative and they like to take it slow.

Doves will appreciate hearing about charitable causes your corporation supports (direct selling U.S. corporations donate more than $100 million to charity every year).

Once they have given you the courtesy of their attention, give doves space and time to make a decision. They do not like taking risks and will want to be certain before they commit. Doves will turn away if they feel you are pressuring them.

How to Keep Doves Motivated

Give doves lots of reassurance and support at the outset and they will grow steadily. They need to feel what they are doing is worthwhile. Follow through on your promises and never forget to call when you said you would. Doves need to be appreciated too, and will respond to mentoring and support. A personal call or note will carry more weight than an e-mail.

Robins

Robins are motivated by a need for acceptance and belonging.

Communal by nature, they are happiest when they're part of a group. Undemanding and adaptable, robins are rarely initiators but are always happy to go with the flow. Although they enjoy being included in social gatherings, they do not need or seek the limelight. They enjoy providing an appreciative audience for more outgoing or dominant personalities.

You are a robin if you are generally cheerful and optimistic about life and place high value on family and friendships. You are a robin if you can be counted on to make a fair contribution to team activities regardless of what is happening in your life. You are a robin if you seek approval and prefer to seek a friend's opinion before making big decisions. You are a robin if you don't like change but you work hard to accommodate the needs of others, even if that means adjusting your own needs.

How Robins Fit the Business

Robins enjoy the social side of network marketing. They are wonderful to have in the business because they are likeable and can adapt to most situations. They are highly accepting of others and make friendships easily.

Robins respond to peer pressure. They want the same as everyone else and will work hard to ensure they don't miss out. Robins are steady and stable. You can count on them staying around once they have found their niche. They have no desire to be superstars, but they blend into most groups as loyal, dependable members. Extreme robins find it hard to function outside the group.

How to Approach Robins

Make them feel wanted. They will be inspired by stories about how you got involved and by testimonials from others in your team. They will be interested in the background of the company and the supportive atmosphere that exists in your team.

Robins will appreciate the opportunity to make new friends and be part of a new group. Be patient. Robins are cautious when it comes to making decisions. Be prepared for them to say they want to discuss the business with family or friends before they commit. If possible, get in first by inviting their partners to be present when you present the opportunity.

How to Keep Robins Motivated

Because robins tend to follow the leader, their performance will depend largely on your leadership and the dynamics that exist in your group. Set an example, and your robin will follow it. Robins respond well to clear guidelines, and once they know what is expected of them, they can hold their own in most situations. Make sure you let them know how much you enjoy having them in your team.

Wrens

Wrens are motivated by security.

Hardworking and courageous, they are consummate survivors and will do whatever it takes to provide for the people closest to them.

Wrens are not particularly social outside their tight-knit family group. They are wary of strangers and tend to be reticent about sharing information about themselves. Intensely private, wrens do not readily seek out friendships, preferring to have one or two confidantes they can rely on. Extreme wrens are loners.

You are a wren if you avoid crowds and would prefer to rent a DVD than go out to a movie theater. You are a wren if you are invited to a party and find yourself thinking of an excuse to say no if the invitation comes from outside your comfort zone. You are a wren if you are happiest with your family around you and you dislike interruptions to your routine. You are a wren if you prefer silence to chatter. You are a wren if you don't have a cell phone (unless you left it somewhere and have forgotten where—in which case you're probably a peacock).

How Wrens Fit the Business

Wrens are homemakers and will work hard to provide for the people they care about. They never disappoint anyone who is counting on them.

Wrens have a wonderful quality known as *street smarts*. Because they have a strong need for security, they get results where others fail. They don't give up easily and will draw on all their resources to achieve their goals. Wrens have a built-in ability to rebound from failure and move on from mistakes. Don't underestimate the wren.

How to Approach Wrens

Wrens are tailor-made for a home-based business but they are not the easiest personalities to approach. Focus on the flexibility that will enable them to blend work and family roles.

Don't let their willingness to listen give you a false sense of security. It can take time to earn a wren's trust, but when you do you will discover a shrewd business sense. Don't overlook the potential of these difficult to pin down recruits.

How to Keep Wrens Motivated

Wrens need little outside stimulation to meet the goals they set for themselves. Whatever it takes, they will do. Their enterprise and initiative will astound you.

Eagles

Eagles are driven by success, status and power.

Ambitious and goal-oriented, eagles were born to win—and to win spectacularly. Eagles know what they want and they don't let anything or anybody get in their way. They make decisions quickly and they delegate effortlessly. They have little time for small talk and can be blunt and to the point, which not everyone can relate to. Eagles are unafraid of conflict. They can be tactless, which can lead to bruised egos and resentment. Extreme eagles are overbearing and confrontational.

Eagles are confident, charismatic, and assertive. They have great faith in themselves and their ability to succeed, whatever the odds. Give them a job and they'll get it done, even though they dislike detail. Eagles are persuasive when they want something and have no qualms about turning up the charm to get their own way. If charm doesn't work, extreme eagles sometimes resort to coercion.

You are an eagle if you are highly competitive. You hate to lose even when the stakes are small. You do not suffer fools gladly and you are impatient when people get in your way. You are an eagle if you cannot bear to wait in line and you speed up when the lights turn yellow. You are an eagle if you name drop (or would if you could) and you have a wallet full of platinum credit cards.

How Eagles Fit the Business

Eagles are social climbers who relish the opportunity to excel in front of their peers. They soak up the recognition that comes with achievement. Their self-confidence is highly persuasive, so they have no trouble attracting recruits. They expect their recruits to perform, but no less than they expect of themselves, so they make great leaders. Their ambition and drive give them a greater-than-average chance of succeeding.

How to Approach Eagles

Make them feel important. Eagles are demanding, status driven, and have supreme confidence. They quickly grasp the potential of the business as a way to achieve what they want in life. Don't waffle, as eagles are impatient. Aim your eagle's sights high. Talk about the rewards that come with the top levels of the plan. Eagles are not interested in modest rewards. They only want the best, and they believe they deserve it without question or hesitation.

How to Keep Eagles Motivated

Eagles are the most self-motivated of all birds. Once eagles make a commitment, their confidence, charisma, and supreme egos will be powerful forces as they build their organization.

Recognition is important to eagles, but tangible rewards excite them more. Exotic trips, late-model cars, jewelry, invitations to VIP events, and trophies they can display as symbols of their success motivate them more than praise. Give eagles a goal, especially one with status attached, and they'll go for it.

Owls

Owls are motivated by the desire for knowledge and understanding.

The wise old owl sat on the oak.

The more he saw the less he spoke.

The less he spoke the more he heard.

Why can't we be like that wise bird?

This children's poem pretty much sums up the owl. Owls are thinkers. Calm, patient, and observant, they are interested in and motivated by detail. Owls can't get enough facts, figures, data, or information. They are orderly and organized, and they hate clutter. Extreme owls are hoarders because they refuse to discard any item that may be useful at a later date. Extreme owls can also be stubborn and overly picky.

Although they have serious natures and may lack social skills, owls remain true to the people they respect. Their analytical, pedantic personalities can sometimes be frustrating (except to other owls), but they are honest, reliable, and hardworking.

You are an owl if you have a tidy sock drawer and you know the exact balance of your checking account. You are an owl if you think the compensation plan is an interesting read. You are an owl if science programs fascinate you and you enjoy solving mathematical problems. You are an owl if you make lists and methodically tick tasks off as you accomplish them. You are an owl if you enjoy playing Sudoku—and the more difficult it is, the more you like it.

How Owls Fit the Business

Owls like being self-employed because it means being in control of their own income. They can see the value of the tax breaks that are part of the deal. Thoughtful and rational, owls will not be talked into anything that cannot be backed up with sound data, but they recognize a good business opportunity when they see it and will apply themselves to make it work.

How to Approach Owls

Owls make decisions based on facts, so do your homework. An owl will ask many questions and expect clear, well-thought-out answers. Talk to them about the income and benefits, such as the monthly car bonus. Owls will be happy to sit through a presentation on the compensation plan and will soon know more about it than you do. The blank look could be a sign that they are thinking it through. Owls are perfectionists. Make sure you follow up exactly when you said you would and never make excuses.

How to Keep Owls Motivated

Be organized. You will not need to remind owls of the benefits of the business or the need to be consistent. They will know where they are heading and how to get there. They may need help with people skills, because owls sometimes underestimate the importance of communication.

Ostriches

Ostriches are motivated by a desire to fit in.

Ostriches are unconventional. Although they want to be somewhere, they tend to be a little hazy when it comes to pinpointing an exact destination.

Slightly out of synch with their environment, ostriches lack coordination and are usually disorganized. When faced with challenges, they are more likely to put their heads in the sand than attempt to control the situation.

These interesting characters are fun to be around and get through life on the strength of their affable personalities. They are never short of friends because they are sociable and they make great storytellers. Generous and trusting by nature, ostriches can get themselves into sticky situations because they are not great judges of character. Friends may find themselves coming to the Ostrich's rescue.

You are an ostrich if your house is untidy and you never remember where you put things. You are an ostrich if you are not good at budgeting and sometimes go into overdraft when you forget to transfer funds to your checking account. You are an ostrich if you tend to procrastinate, especially when it comes to making important decisions. You are an ostrich if you never make lists, or you make them and forget them.

Extreme ostriches are misfits who struggle to find their niche in life. While eagles make things happen and robins wait for things to happen, ostriches spend their lives wondering what happened.

How Ostriches Fit the Business

Network marketing is a friendly, supportive environment for ostriches. They are not good at setting goals, so they appreciate the guidelines in the compensation plan. Ostriches enjoy the social and personal growth benefits that are part of the package.

Entrepreneurial and imaginative, ostriches enjoy the flexibility of the business. They are not great problem solvers, so the support of an understanding sponsor can make all the difference to their performance. In return their generous, optimistic natures make them popular members of any team.

How to Approach Ostriches

If there are few ostriches in network marketing, it is because no one thinks to approach them. Don't judge by appearances or underestimate their potential because they appear somewhat unconventional. Good listeners, they will be interested in what you share with them and pleased you believe they have what it takes to succeed. Ostriches are eager to achieve and will appreciate the opportunity network marketing offers.

How to Keep Ostriches Motivated

Ostriches need patience and guidance. Give them short-term tasks rather than setting long-terms goals. They can easily veer off course, so keep a close watch on their progress. You don't want them missing out on a promotion because they misunderstood or misread the fine print. Cultivate a sense of humor and don't allow yourself to be frustrated when things go awry.

Cuckoos

Cuckoos are motivated by the desire for an easy life.

In the wild, cuckoos lay their eggs in nests built by other birds. Human cuckoos share the same irresponsible, selfish traits. They are happy to let others do all the work so they can have a free ride. They seize every chance to get something for nothing and have no conscience about taking advantage of others.

How Cuckoos Fit the Business

Cuckoos are too lazy for network marketing. They may fit in for a short time because they can be charming when they want something, but their unwillingness to contribute and their reliance on other people's good natures will quickly cause resentment.

How to Approach Cuckoos

You are better off without them.

Vultures

Vultures are motivated by greed.

Unscrupulous predators, they seize every opportunity to take advantage of others. Anyone who appears weaker is fair game.

How Vultures Fit the Business

Vultures are happy to succeed at the expense of others. They are the antithesis of the people we need in network marketing.

How to Approach Vultures

Keep your distance.

Crows

Crows are motivated by a desire to dominate.

How Crows Fit the Business

Aggressive, intelligent, and controlling, they are bullies who aggressively exploit others without conscience or compassion. Crows in your team will scare away genuine network marketers.

How to Approach Crows

Don't even think about it.

Swans

Swans are motivated by personal growth.

Beautiful, elegant, and gracious swans didn't start that way. They started out as ugly ducklings. Swans have big dreams, but their low self-esteem stops them from achieving their dreams. They yearn for success and they admire anyone who is successful. The problem is they have difficulty seeing themselves as achievers. Many have been let down or put down by others and secretly believe they are unworthy or unqualified to rise above their current situation.

Honest and hardworking, swans have all the ingredients for success except a belief in themselves. Extreme swans are timid and withdrawn.

You are a swan if you loved fairy tales as a child. You are a swan if you see the best in others but are surprised and even embarrassed when you receive compliments. You are a swan if you are emotional and easily hurt. You are a swan if you love to daydream and harbor secret dreams of being rescued. You are a swan if you underestimate your looks or doubt your intelligence, even when the evidence suggests otherwise.

How Swans Fit the Business

Network marketing is perfect for swans and swans are perfect for network marketing. They have incredible potential and will flourish with training and encouragement. Whatever their background, skills, or education, swans have a chance to grow more than they ever believed possible. When they succeed, they will be living proof that this business can change lives.

How to Approach Swans

Swans may appear unmotivated, but that is because they have grown a protective shell as a defense against disappointment.

Take it gently, but let them know you think they have what it takes. Your belief in them may be the chance they have been waiting for. Make sure you share personal success stories, especially rags-to-riches stories that demonstrate many of the top income earners came from modest backgrounds.

How to Keep Swans Motivated

Responsive and appreciative, swans will do anything to live up to your expectations. They won't let you down. They will do anything to win your approval and they will soak up everything you teach them. Swans never forget the people who believe in them and help them overcome their feelings of unworthiness.

Although it may be harder to win their trust, and they may need more mentoring than others, swans are worth the effort. They represent the best of what this business is about, and when they succeed beyond their wildest dreams, they will become role models for every swan waiting in the wings for his or her chance to shine.

Turkeys

Turkeys represent every prospect who declines your wonderful network marketing opportunity! Just kidding—but if it helps you cope with rejection, you have my permission to think it.

What Is Your Personality?

By now, you will have good idea of your personality type. You will also be learning about your friends, family, and team members. Perhaps you have had several ah-ha moments when you realized why they think and act the way they do.

As you worked out your own personality type, you probably discovered you share traits with two or more birds. Most people see themselves as a hybrid. Your true personality is the dominant one, although many of us are a combination of two. If you think you fit all the profiles, you are a probably a peacock. See what I mean? It's all about you.

Not everyone is an extreme personality type. Imagine a scale between one (a few similarities) and five (just about everything applies to you). If you are unsure, number each bird from one to five according to how closely your personality matches. Narrow your choices down as much as you can, while keeping in mind that the more extreme your personality traits, the less likely it is you are a combo.

Take into account that we call on different behaviors to fit different situations. Being a parent may bring out the dove in us, and we call on our eagle traits when we are in positions of authority. At a party, the peacock emerges, and at a family gathering when our elder siblings take charge, we display the characteristics of a robin. In times of adversity, we may pull up the drawbridge and behave like wrens or become a dove and use our misfortune as a turning point to help others even less fortunate.

Some people mask their true nature to achieve an objective, for example, to win friends or approval. The true personality will emerge eventually, usually triggered by stressful, unexpected, or unfamiliar situations. This makes the process of identifying the personalities of others a little more challenging but a lot more interesting.

The characteristics of some birds cannot be combined, because they are opposites. If you are an eagle, your dove traits will be overwhelmed by your ambition. If you are a social peacock, you can't be a reclusive wren as well. However, peacocks can have eagle tendencies and eagles can have owl tendencies.

But here is the key. This is not about you. The key to recruiting by personality is learning to identify and adapt to your prospects.

For example, pretend you are a fast-talking, enthusiastic peacock and your prospect is a data-hungry owl. Facts are not your forte, but you know they will be important to your prospect.

Arrive at the interview armed with facts, figures, and statistics. Hold your tongue. Fast talkers do not impress cautious owls. Tone down your enthusiasm, and pause often to give your owl time to think about what you are saying. Let the owl ask questions. Don't put pressure on owls to sign or you may lose them. They will respect you for giving them time to decide what they want to do.

If you are an eagle, coming on too strong will scare away the robins and doves you need to build your organization. That's if you notice them. If you don't, who loses? You!

If you are an owl, understand that not everyone shares your fascination for the intricate details of the compensation plan. If your prospects' eyes are glazing over or they start fidgeting, stop explaining and start asking questions.

The quicker you learn to identify and adapt to your prospect's personality, the sooner you will build your organization. If you are unsure about a prospect, or anyone for that matter, trust your intuition. You may have a hunch about someone, change your mind, and then discover your first impression was right all along. The more you understand what makes other people tick, the more you will go with your gut and avoid investing time and energy in the wrong people.

The easiest trap to fall into as you build your organization is looking for people like yourself. Although it is easier to establish rapport with like minds, smart recruiters reach out to a broader spectrum. If you have a hot prospect who is everything you are not, think about asking someone with a better chance of creating empathy to help you present the business to this person. Perhaps a smart move would be to involve your sponsor in the process or to use tools more likely to spark the prospect's interest in the business.

Team dynamics do matter. A balanced team will produce better results because everyone gets the benefit of a wider range of outlook and talents. If you focus one or two personality types, you will limit your growth.

CHAPTER SEVENTEEN

Why Your Business Will Appeal to Achievers

SURROUNDING YOURSELF WITH ACHIEVERS is a smart strategy. Don't become starstruck or let nerves stop you from approaching respected leaders in your community and people you admire.

You will fast-track your growth if you recruit people with a track record of success. They have proved they have what it takes to succeed, and their talents and skills will carry over into their network marketing business.

Not all achievers earn as much as they should. According to the U.S. Census Bureau, nearly one-third of Americans older than age twenty-five have at least a bachelor's degree and earn on average $52,000 a year. Those with advanced degrees earn around $80,000. Although that is considered a reasonable income in the workforce, it is not as high as the six-figure incomes earned by the top achievers in network marketing.

The way the U.S. economy is changing does not bode well for achievers. The skilled jobs are disappearing and the middle class is shrinking. There are many reasons why the trend is irreversible.

Globalization

White-collar jobs are disappearing offshore at a faster rate every year. Manufacturing jobs are flowing out of the United States and into China, India, Russia, and South America. As India's middle class is rising, the U.S. middle class is falling.

In California—the fifth largest economy in the world—fewer than 30 percent of workers are classified as middle-class earners. Apart from a few wealthy individuals, the rest are low-paid workers.

The technology sector is heading offshore hot on the heels of manufacturing. Virtual offices are replacing downtown office towers. Web-development work that charged out at $100 an hour five years ago can now be bought for $5 an hour from a third-world country—with no reduction in the quality of work.

Closed-circuit television is replacing doctors in the operating room, and more and more Americans are choosing to have elective surgery overseas. When they return home mended, they boast of hospitals resembling resorts, red-carpet treatment, and first-class medical attention.

Outsourcing is understandable. It increases profits, so the top echelon of CEOs gets richer. Meanwhile, highly skilled workers in the United States get poorer as they compete for fewer jobs.

Competition

Education is no guarantee of a top job anymore. The future will see more graduates competing with people from other countries who have equal education and skills but will work for less.

Automation

Everywhere you look, machines are replacing people. Bank clerks have morphed into ATM machines. Air travelers print boarding passes before they leave home or at an automated booth in the airport. Touch-screen kiosks are popping up at eateries across the United States, and shoppers are checking out their own groceries at supermarkets. Robots have replaced real people on customer service lines, and 800 numbers are answered anywhere but in the United States. We print our own coupons, stamps, and tickets, and we book online, pay our bills online, and manage our bank accounts online. This all adds up to a high tally of lost jobs for skilled workers.

Productivity

According to some surveys, the average worker wastes eighty-seven days a year in nonproductive activity, such as making personal calls, surfing the Internet, sending e-mails, daydreaming, taking sick days, dawdling in the restroom, and sneaking off for a cigarette break. It adds up to more than one workday a week for every worker—down the drain!

If you are motivated and industrious—and working for someone else—you are compensating for coworkers who are not pulling their weight. Employers have to factor in good workers and bad when they calculate salaries. That means half the workers (the slackers) are paid more than they are worth and half (the performers) are paid less than they are worth.

Motivated workers, the very people we want in this industry, are subsidizing their lazy, inefficient coworkers. It doesn't seem fair, and it isn't. But brooding about it won't change a thing.

Unless you are the CEO of a large corporation, becoming self-employed is just about the only way to ensure you are paid what you are worth. Achievers are ripe for recruiting into our reward-for-results business.

It's time to give achievers the ammunition they need to fire their employers.

Talk to every skilled worker you know about how to start a business by working just ten hours a week. After one year, they will have invested five hundred hours in their business. Then let them decide if they want to leave their jobs and work their business full-time or continue part-time to top up their regular income. Either way, they will have more to spend and a better shot at retiring with a healthier investment portfolio.

Ask productive workers if their employers pay for their annual vacations. After they have stopped laughing, they will tell you they can't afford to travel and are under increasing pressure to forfeit at least some of their vacation time.

Go-getters don't leave the office—they take it with them. Workers have become so addicted to their Blackberries, they've become known as "Crackberries."

Show your prospects photos of your annual vacation at an exotic resort and explain that it cost you nothing. Sure, you had to achieve it, but think about how many hours you worked to reach your vacation target. I will be surprised if it was a full forty-hour-week effort.

Ask your prospects if their employers are covering their car lease payments. Explain how your car is or will be a perk of your job as long as you reach and maintain your monthly target.

Don't keep your business a secret from achievers. Anyone with ambition and a good work ethic is a leading candidate for a network marketing business.

According to a survey conducted by the Direct Selling Association, 35 percent of direct sellers are college graduates, and 8 percent have postgraduate degrees. There is a rising swell of achievers joining the business, so make sure you don't miss the wave.

The smarter you are and the more ambitious you are, the more you should avoid working for someone else. Technology allows self-employed entrepreneurs to run their small businesses with all the resources of a large one. Wireless technology means you can run a business from any place, including your vacation home in Florida or a resort in Mexico, and still look professional. You can also choose when to turn off—you're the boss!

The twenty-first century brought in a new attitude. Self-employment used to be considered the risky option. Now working for a corporation is considered far riskier.

This change has not been lost on big corporations like Time Warner, Jockey, Virgin, Berkshire Hathaway, Unilever, Hallmark, L'Oreal, Nestle, and Mars, which have all started or invested in direct selling divisions.

The IRS has recognized the mind shift by changing the tax laws. Self-employed people now have access to the same benefits as employees (more if you count the tax breaks that come with a home office).

You have so much to offer the highest achievers in the United States. Topping the list is flexibility. Achievers have what it takes to succeed in any area they choose, but they will pay a lower personal price for success if they are self-employed.

Now we're talking the American dream.

CHAPTER EIGHTEEN

Helping Gen Ys Realize Their Dreams

IF YOU WERE BORN BETWEEN 1980 and 1994, you belong to the most powerful emerging consumer group in the world. You make up over one fifth of the population of the United States, Australia, Canada, and Great Britain. You account for more than half of the entire population of India and there are more of you in China than the entire population of the United States.

If you were not born in that era, you can't afford to overlook the incredible clout of young people. According to *USA Today*, "Generation Y sits on top of the consumer food chain."

In just a few short years, they grew MySpace to more than 160 million users and turned YouTube into a 24/7 political, societal, and media watchdog, Google into the world's largest reference library, and Technorati into the world's largest chat room.

What drives them? Communication, innovation, and instant gratification.

These young adults are hot and more diverse than any former generation in the history of the United States. Over a third of them are Hispanic, African, Native American, or Asian American and one in four of them come from single-parent households. Seventy-five percent grew up with a working mother.

Gen Ys have burst onto the employment scene like no generation before. Brought up by nurturing, highly communicative parents, they are confident, creative, and more than a little cocky. Accustomed to masses of support and feedback from nurturing parents, they demand recognition and respect as a right.

Highly educated and supremely ambitious, they bring a wealth of skills to the workforce and they plan to use them to advance themselves. Their high expectations are matched only by their impatience to reach the top of whatever career they choose. They expect their needs to be accommodated, whether it's relaxed dress codes or time off to pursue their own interests.

Corporations trapped in outdated ideologies are struggling to adapt to these free-spirited individuals. The rules have changed, and traditional employers are reeling. Blanket policies—such as no tattoos or body piercing—make little sense when 50 percent of all twenty to thirty-year-olds have a tattoo or piercing somewhere other than their earlobes. No longer a statement of rebellion, tattoos have become a must-have Gen Y fashion accessory. The change makes many employers uneasy.

Having their decisions questioned is only one of the challenges CEOs face. Holding on to their employees is another. Gen Ys are restless and more than willing to switch jobs for better pay or conditions. Researchers predict a typical Gen Y will average twenty-nine jobs in five different industries over his or her lifetime.

The grass is definitely greener on our side of the fence. Ambitious, entrepreneurial, and eager to take responsibility for their financial future, Gen Ys are prime candidates to start their own businesses.

Our reward-for-results culture is uniquely positioned to appeal to them.

✴ They seek freedom and flexibility. They will find all the freedom they need in network marketing.

* They refuse to let work get in the way of social and leisure pursuits. They will appreciate being able to control their time and schedule.

* They insist on recognition and respect. Every success and milestone will be celebrated.

* They thrive on feedback and support. As their sponsor, you will be a willing mentor.

* They are idealists who want to make a worthwhile contribution. Network marketing will give them the opportunity to change many lives.

* They respond to learning. They will make great students and teachers as they learn and pass on skills.

* They are adaptable. They will not be deterred by the roller-coaster ride that is network marketing.

* They fit well into a team environment. They are tailormade for our knowledge-sharing culture.

* They are easily bored.

* They are used to being stimulated and entertained.

Network marketing is life accelerated. No two days are the same and nothing is ever certain or predictable. And we build fun into the business.

The only barrier holding Gen Ys back from their ambitious dreams will be their own limitations. Energy and exuberance will compensate for their lack of experience if you present them with a challenge that excites.

These young adults are your future business builders. The question is, where do you find them and how do you approach them?

The *where* part is easy. As they represent almost one in every four Americans, you would have to make an effort to miss them. Take a fresh look at the younger members of your friends and family (eighteen is the minimum age to sign an agreement).

Head for the mall on a Saturday. Browse in shops catering

to young shoppers, such as music, electronics, computer, and fashion stores. Get in line at McDonald's or Starbucks. Hang out at the beach, the park, or the lake. Go to concerts, and participate in career days on campuses. Take a booth at a bridal expo. Any-where and everywhere young people hang out, you'll find your Gen Y prospects.

Unless you are a member of the Gen Y club, in which case connecting will come naturally, the *how* part will take a little more enterprise.

★   First, you have to catch their attention. They are media savvy, and they have a healthy skepticism for outdated and irrele-vant messages. They are also easily distracted, so you'll have to make it stimulating. This generation has unlimited volumes of information at their fingertips. They'll check anything they want to know online in seconds, so be on your toes.

★   If they are working, they may be discovering the restric-tions that come with a regular job. Here's a message you can use to your advantage: Experts predict this will be the first generation destined to earn less than their parents. The only way they will break that pattern is if they can find a career that will accommo-date their restless spirit.

★   If they are studying, you can offer a part-time job with many benefits. It pays well, it's flexible enough to accommodate classes, and it's an opportunity to gain work experience. Future employers will be impressed by résumés that demonstrate experi-ence and initiative, but with luck, their time with you will inspire Gen Ys to stick with their network marketing business.

★   Consider offering students an internship over the sum-mer. Thousands of students put themselves through college every year that way. What better way to learn business skills than on the job? What are the odds they will decide to stay with you when they realize the freedom they will lose if they go corporate?

★   If you have a specific line designed for a younger demo-graphic—such as telecommunications, Internet services, all-in-one nutritional products, fashion clothing, or cosmetics and accessories—you have an easy opener:

> "I am looking for people to promote a product line we have developed for twenty- to thirty-year-olds. Have you heard of [your company name]?"

If the answer is yes, then ask:

> "Have you seen our new look?"

And on you go.
If the answer is no, then ask:

> "Do you have five minutes to help me with a survey I am conducting? I only want to speak to young people."

★ Fashion, skin care, cosmetics, hair products and jewelry lend themselves to promotion through an event such as a fashion show or new-season expo. Ask young people—daughters, nieces, babysitters, or young neighbors—to hand out flyers and text friends to promote your event. Motivate and reward them with a chance to model your products.

★ You won't make new contacts at home. Book a venue in an area you want to target and walk a few blocks around it handing out flyers to young prospects. Add an irresistible offer such as the chance to win free products. Young people love free stuff! Ask people to "bring a couple of friends." Your social Gen Y prospects are much more likely to turn up if they can come as a pack.

★ If your company does not have an age-specific line, ask prospects for their advice about how to appeal to a younger age group. Young people know what they like. Don't try to second-guess them. An hour of quality listening will yield a wealth of valuable feedback you can use.

★ Consider running a seminar for graduates or school

leavers on how to start a business. Or sponsor an event targeted to young people. Speak on campus. Young people make brilliant audiences and you can count on tons of interaction and lively debate.

✯   Get serious. Make sure you can communicate on their wavelength. Learning to text is a basic. These young people are not waiting at home for the phone to ring, and e-mail is snail mail to them. Seventy percent of Americans have a cell phone before they reach their teens. Your text message will reach them wherever they are, and they will not be able to resist opening it.

✯   Talk now! Gen Ys thinks the world ends at age thirty, so focus on how they can earn money today—for the next Play-Station, Nintendo Wii, cool car, surfboard, or entertainment. You may think Gen Ys need to start planning for their future but that's your perspective talking, not theirs. Zip your lip if you're tempted to venture beyond the zone they inhabit.

✯   Be yourself—if you are not a Gen Y member, don't mess up your chance to connect by making ill-fated attempts to look or speak younger than you are. Trying to imitate their look or vocabulary will make you appear foolish. Your prospects will listen to you if you apply the principles outlined in this book.

✯   Gen Ys have grown up with countless stories about young people starting businesses in garages or basements and going on to make loads of money. They don't have the same self-doubt issues other generations have.

You may find your Gen Y prospects already have an eye out for an entrepreneurial opportunity. Be prepared to compete for them. They will head straight to their PCs to compare your opportunity with others.

If you are successful in encouraging them to sign, you will need to be on your toes. This impatient lot will want to seek quick results, but they are optimistic and fearless when it comes to getting what they want. Give them lots of direction, feedback, and recognition and you will get your future residuals.

CHAPTER NINETEEN

Helping Gen Xs Get What They Want

NEARLY 50 MILLION AMERICANS carry the tag "Gen X." They were born in the late sixties and throughout the seventies, and they are the 4M generation. They're married, mortgaged, mothers—and they need money.

These spoiled children of baby boomer parents grew up surrounded by material comforts. They're used to having it all. Their problem is how to pay for it, which makes them hot prospects.

Chances are they work, but their modest wages aren't enough to cover household expenses. They want a nice home, a decent car, all the luxuries their parents had—and more. Their children want brand-name clothes, the latest toys, and expect to go to college. The cost of education is skyrocketing. Annual tuition, fees, room, and board at a four-year college start at $13,000, and private universities run upward of $30,000.

This household is strapped for cash. It can't be run on a single income.

Your opportunity is tailor-made for Gen Xs, especially young mothers. While the husband continues his regular job to pay the bills, the wife can start a business to provide the extras they are missing out on.

She can be at home for the children when they need her, and she can build her business while they are at school. He can baby-sit nights and weekends.

Money is not the only motivator. Many Gen Xs married straight out of school. Their children are gaining independence and they are ready to start spreading their wings. This may be their first chance to pursue dreams they postponed to buy a house and start a family.

Network marketing is not new to this group. Hosting and attending parties is already part of their lives and they most likely have a friend, neighbor, or close family member in the business.

Some Gen Xs grew up with parents who were network mar-keters. This is both good and bad—good if they have had first-hand experience of the benefits of the business; bad if they are carrying outdated perceptions.

Network marketing has undergone an amazing transforma-tion in recent years.

Their parents may have spent half their time collating orders and placing them by fax, phone, or mail; tracking team results manually; and packing and delivering customer orders. They didn't have access to online ordering, direct shipping, wireless credit card terminals, and duplicate checks. Personal websites, e-mails, and cell phones weren't invented yet.

Despite the relatively unsophisticated nature of the business, their parents succeeded, many of them spectacularly. Think what motivated people who are free to spend 100 percent of their time at the front lines of their businesses can achieve today!

Many Gen Xs grew up as latchkey kids, with both parents working in corporate jobs. They have seen the price their parents paid to work outside the home and are determined not to make the same mistake.

Introduce your Gen X prospects to the "new face" of net-work marketing. Talk to them about downloadable resources, e-communications, and auto-shipping. Talk about Web conferencing and having a virtual office linked directly to the corporation.

Start your Gen X recruiting campaign by positioning yourself where Gen Xs congregate. Trade shows, expos, and events specifically targeting women are starters. Young moms will be meeting their friends in coffee shops, at the playground, or at the mall on weekdays. They'll be gathering at day care centers, mother-and-child events run by church and community groups, and participating in early childhood support groups.

When talking with people from this group, plant seeds that directly address the issues they care about—money, children, and personal growth.

> "The best part of this business is being able to spend time with my family but also having time to myself, doing what I love doing."
>
> "Being able to have my own business and be at home with my kids is great. This job has given me the life I want—and the money to pay for it!"

Talk about the training. Your Gen X prospects are thirsty for new skills and hungry for the chance to develop their talents.

Most husbands will be happy to babysit when they see the impact the business can have on the household income and on their partners' self-esteem and confidence. Many will be itching to take an active role in the business.

Tempt your prospects with the trips and incentives they can work toward. Rewards are often more motivating than money to self-indulgent Gen Xs. Few will be able to resist a break from their routines to join in the fun and excitement of an annual convention.

Moms are sorely overlooked in the recognition stakes. This could be her chance to shine in the spotlight. Show her photos of the annual awards banquet, the recognition pins, and the trophies. Don't forget to mention the monthly car payments, free vacations at luxury resorts, and jewelry up for grabs.

You will have a jump start if you represent products your prospects are already using. Toys, educational games, books, casual clothes, pet care, health and beauty products are top sellers, while candles and home decorative products are winners for this house-proud group. High-ticket items like air purifiers and water filters, and savings on utilities will appeal to Gen Xs furnishing their homes on a budget.

This group has the advantage of a wide circle of contacts to call on. Their friends will be at a similar stage in their lives and wide open to an approach to join the business. Peer pressure doesn't stop at high school.

Appeal to their social conscience by talking about the contribution your company makes to charitable causes. Gen Xs have a strong sense of community.

You will find more ideas in Chapter Eleven, but widen your scope beyond married couples. Many women are postponing marriage until their thirties. A significant percentage is single or newly single after a divorce. Women who rely solely on their husbands' income are highly vulnerable after a split. A small business could provide their security.

One in six Americans belongs to the Gen X club. Gen Xers know what they want and they are finding out how much it costs. Make sure you are there when they are looking for a way to get it.

CHAPTER TWENTY

Brightening the Future for Baby Boomers

THE 78 MILLION BABY BOOMERS born between 1946 and 1964 are the largest and most powerful consumer group ever. Their estimated annual spending power is $2 trillion!

Where is the money going? Baby boomers are spending up large to pamper themselves and to spoil their kids and their grandchildren. Your opportunity is a perfect fit for the issues they care about—lifestyle, retirement, and health care.

If you represent health products, your earnings could go through the roof by recruiting this group. We already spend $250 per person a year on nutritional supplements, and the trend is fueled by a growing skepticism of the "manage the symptoms" approach favored by drug companies. The catastrophic side effects of several widely used drugs have deepened the distrust. As manufacturers are sacrificing nutrition for foods that are brighter in color, easier to prepare, and have longer shelf lives, the nutritional industry will continue its rapid growth.

Baby boomers are taking back responsibility for their health by switching to a prevention philosophy based on nutritional supplementation.

That's not all. Baby boomers have no intention of aging gracefully. Skin and hair-care products, especially anti-aging formulas, are set to explode over the next few years.

Just about every product sold by direct sellers will appeal to this group—in addition to skin-care and healthcare products, they need pet care, gardening, home décor, cleaning products, and clothing for themselves. They'll be interested in cookware, scrapbooking, and essential oils as gifts for their adult children. They'll be interested in giving their grandchildren books, crafts, educational programs, and toys.

Why will this group buy direct? In a word—service! Baby boomers value personal over automated service. These spare-no-expense prospects could transform your business, because there's a catch.

The catch is that the spending power is concentrated in the hands of the wealthiest baby boomers. Although a few are awash with money, the rest are struggling to stay afloat.

Nearly two out of three baby boomers admit to worrying about retirement, and most expect to continue working beyond age sixty-five. The IRS estimates that only 4 percent of baby boomers will be financially secure at age sixty-five, and a mere 1 percent will be wealthy.

Inflation has been running ahead of cost-of-living increases for at least five years and there is little sign of the trend being reversed. Healthcare costs continue to escalate and Medicare won't be the panacea many believe it will. Baby boomers will be shocked to discover they could face monthly top-up contributions of $100 or more once income adjustments, supplemental coverage, and prescription drug plans are factored in. Some married couples could be paying more than $3,000 a year on top of Medicare.

Anti-aging advances compound the problem even further. Life expectancy is rising an extra year, every year. There is little chance retirees will be supported by government programs at current levels.

There is a lot at stake, and what a better way to brighten the outlook for the 95 percent of baby boomers who need money than starting a home-based business?

Talk to baby boomers ASAP. Explain that supplementing their income with a part-time job and investing the profits for their retirement could prevent them from falling into the poverty trap.

Your presentation will not fall on deaf ears. According to American Association of Retired Persons (AARP), 77 percent of baby boomers plan to work after the age of sixty-five. It won't be in the careers they have now, because traditional employers will replace them with younger models.

Baby boomers already account for nearly half of self-employed workers according to the U.S. Department of Labor, and this will grow as more retire or get laid off from their regular jobs.

Your business could be a lifesaver. The average credit card debt of Americans sixty-five and older is $5,000. Their homes are mortgaged. Even if they are paid off, a $250,000 home is a lousy retirement policy. A reverse mortgage means kissing good-bye to the kids' inheritance, and polls indicate baby boomers have a strong desire to leave money for future generations.

The key point is that baby boomers' options are limited. Your fifties is not a good time to invest capital in a risky or unproven business venture. Baby boomers have less time to recover from failure. A network marketing business doesn't involve risk.

The fact that so many baby boomers are financially ill equipped for retirement is a potential boon for your opportunity. They have the motivation, fewer family commitments to work around, and job skills to transfer to a business. Tapping into their pursuit of a fulfilling lifestyle will ensure a steady flow of baby boomers into your organization for years to come.

CHAPTER TWENTY-ONE

Women and Network Marketing

CAN YOU RECALL AN EXACT TIME when you knew your life was about to veer off course?

Mine was graduation day, as I was about to realize my dream of becoming a teacher. My mother-in-law had been very supportive in helping me care for my baby daughter while I studied and had offered to continue while I taught school.

But something felt different, and it took all of five minutes to recognize that unmistakable sensation. I was pregnant again.

"This won't change anything," I reasoned, half believing it. Although I was going to have to juggle more balls, and juggle them faster and higher, I was young, fit, and capable. I could do it.

My first year of teaching was a haze. After taking six weeks off when my son was born, I returned to the classroom to honor my promise to complete the year with my students. But the writing was on the wall. My teaching days were numbered.

I began scanning the local paper for a job that would pay the bills but give me time to spend with my children. On the help-wanted page, three magic words leapt at me: *work from home!*

Within seconds, I was on the phone and was granted an interview the same afternoon. It lasted only a few minutes before—and you are not going to believe this—I got the job.

Okay, now I get it. But at the time I was an accidental network marketer. Like so many women, I stumbled into it with little understanding of how it worked.

And, like nine out of ten of us, I signed up with small, short-term goals—to pay the mortgage until my children were old enough for me to return to teaching.

I had a rocky start. My self-confidence was below zero, so I wore long skirts at my parties so people wouldn't see my knees shaking. I discriminated against anyone who looked like a great prospect, assuming she wouldn't be interested. Even if she was, I lacked the confidence to approach her.

It took a few months to realize I had stumbled into a career that could literally change my life.

Network marketing meant I could be a great mom to my kids, I could help pay the bills, and I could enjoy a life most people only dream about—all at the same time.

Network marketing tops the list of career choices for women. No job comes close to matching it.

Single, married, separated, divorced, or widowed, the chips are seriously stacked against women in the financial stakes. The U.S. Census Bureau reports women earn seventy-five cents for doing the same job a man is paid a dollar to do.

The more educated women are, the worse they fare. According to figures compiled by the Department of Education, one year out of college women earn 80 percent as much as their male counterparts. Each year the disparity stretches. Ten years out of college, they're earning only 69 percent.

Women contribute more than half the family income in 55 percent of households, but you don't find these alpha earners in corporations. Out of all the Fortune 500 corporations, a measly thirteen have female CEOs. Four out of five have no women anywhere near the top echelons.

Where are the alpha earners? They're in entrepreneurial en-terprises like network marketing where the majority of high-income earners are women. Every woman who reaches the top level is helping other women work up to join her. There is always room for more at the top in our industry, and the only way to reach it is to help others succeed. Compare that to the competi-tive environment that marks most workplaces.

If you are one of the twenty-five thousand women who start a network marketing business every day in the United States, shout it from the rooftops. And be very loud, so other women can hear you. Encourage career women to stop swimming against the corporate tide and to start building their own pool. Encour-age young women to consider network marketing as a first choice of career, not as a fallback job when they marry, have children, or lose faith in the corporate system.

Tell them, "In network marketing, you will be paid on the basis of your performance, not your sex," and "the majority of high-income earners are women."

It is not just about high fliers. Talk to the women who hold jobs well below their skills, experience, and education after taking a break to raise a family. Talk to all the women who work in low-paid, low-satisfaction jobs in shops, offices, and factories. Offer them a chance to escape from the nine-to-five drudgery to a busi-ness that is profitable, energizing, and fun. Life is too short to toil in a dull job where you will be underappreciated and underpaid.

Anyone who has raised a family has management skills. Any-one who runs a home has organizational skills. Women are tailor-made to become network marketers. We thrive on multitasking, and the skills needed to succeed—sharing, building relationships, and nurturing—are second nature to us. We instinctively do what needs to be done.

Women already own 40 percent of all private businesses and 70 percent of all start-ups, but cost can dissuade many women entrepreneurs from starting their own business.

Let your prospects know that in network marketing the corporation invests in them. Explain how little a starter kit costs and that the corporation contributes products, training, and support of far greater value. Tell them they risk nothing when they start, and if it's not the right fit, they can walk away having lost nothing.

Talk to married women. Marriage is no free pass to financial freedom. Spouses lose their jobs or take pay cuts. Divorce rates are skyrocketing, and the average age of widowhood in America is fifty-five. Twenty percent of all home buyers are unmarried women, according to the Joint Center for Housing Studies at Harvard University. Women who work are better equipped to manage when things go sour—no question.

Talk to single women. Running a small business can be lonely. In network marketing, you're in business for yourself but not by yourself. You will have support on a daily basis and many opportunities to swap ideas and gain friends and inspiration at training meetings, at conventions, and on incentive vacations.

Network marketing may be the best-kept secret in the United States and there has never been a better time to spread the word—loud and proud!

CHAPTER TWENTY-TWO

Men and Network Marketing

JUST BECAUSE 80 PERCENT of network marketers are women doesn't make it an exclusive women-only club.

The diversification of products and services available though direct selling channels is changing men's attitudes to the business. Edgy nutritional supplements, wine, coffee, chocolate, credit cards, long-distance calling plans, insurance, and legal services are opening the doors to a demographic that has been slow to recognize the potential of network marketing.

That was then, this is now! Across the board, from college graduates with no intention of ever working for someone else to men who are disillusioned by the traditional employment route, men are flowing into the industry.

Products are not the only drawing card. The Internet has created a wealth of opportunities for men in network marketing. Compensation plans now encourage and reward global recruiting. The mind-boggling potential of emerging markets in China, Russia, and India is attracting a new wave of network marketing entrepreneurs. Your opportunity could prove irresistible to men with an adventurous spirit.

Closer to home, traditional employment channels are drying up, which increases competition and makes for a more stressful workplace. Who can blame men for looking for alternative ways to achieve financial freedom?

The United States is harsh on its workers. The Organization for Economic Cooperation and Development (OECD) reports the average American in full-time employment works nearly two thousand hours a year and has just two weeks of vacation.

According to the Center for Economic and Policy Research, the United States is the only advanced economy in the world that does not guarantee its workers paid vacations. One out of ten full-time workers and six out of ten part-time workers get no vacation. Zero. Zip. Zilch. Workers whose jobs do come with paid vacation time take on average just twelve days. Add the commute to every workday and you realize how little time the average worker spends with family and friends.

According to Warren Farrell, the author of *Why Men Earn More*, men who work forty to sixty hours a week are the least fulfilled of all employment groups, while women working part-time at home are the most content. To borrow a popular quote, "No one ever dies wishing they had spent more time at the office."

Imagine cutting your workweek in half and taking four weeks of vacation to relax and recharge. Factor in the time saved not having to commute to the office, and you almost triple the time available to enjoy family, friends, and leisure pursuits.

How do you attract more men to the business?

Making decisions about career and finances is a big deal for men. The benefits of your business—that is, the difference between what they have and what they want—have to carry enough punch to make them sit up and take notice. Choose from the following approaches:

★   Big benefits eclipse small obstacles. Survey your prospects to find out what they're missing out on in their lives, whether it's family time, leisure time, job satisfaction, or money, and show them how they can have it.

★ Talk to fathers about the childhood memories they want their kids to carry with them throughout their lives. What presence do they want in those memories? No dad wants to be a stranger to his kids. Challenge men who work ridiculous hours or spend weeks away from home on business trips to consider what they really want. You'll strike a chord with someone questioning the sacrifice he makes putting work ahead of family.

★ Ask sports lovers to picture themselves on a surf-ski in Jamaica, a deep-sea fishing expedition off the Florida coast, or a golf course in Maui. Ask business travelers when they last took their wives on a business trip. Talk about how vacations are built into your business. Ask them to imagine walking out onto the balcony of a resort overlooking the ocean, and to picture it all being paid for by their corporate partner. You're not offering them a free ride. They will have to earn their rewards. But you have to work hard to succeed in any job. Most don't come with free vacations, monthly car payments, and a host of performance incentives attached.

★ Look for small-business owners who are plowing all their profits back into the business to keep it afloat. Compare their risks, responsibilities, and returns to yours.

★ Look for men in role-reversal relationships. Men with a partner who is pursuing a corporate career may be wide open to a home-based business, especially if kids are involved. You won't be breaking new ground. There are already men waiting at the school gate.

★ Ask every man this question. "What is the highlight of your day?" If he answers "quitting time," a white-hot prospect has just identified himself.

In the past, women were drawn to network marketing because of circumstances. It was a woman's job to raise the family even if it meant putting her career on the back burner. It was the husband's job to provide a regular source of income. For many men, that meant putting dreams aside. Times are changing. Men are realizing self-reliance is the best security in life and that family comes first.

Offer men an opportunity to take their lives back. You double your prospect base if you offer men the chance to benefit from your incredible business opportunity.

CHAPTER TWENTY-THREE

Recruiting Couples

MANY DOORS OPEN INTO THIS BUSINESS and your prospects could enter through any of them.

One door with a huge POTENTIAL sign on it is marked COUPLES. The industry abounds with couples who have built businesses together. The future will see increasing numbers of network marketers choosing to work the business as a partnership.

Why? Because the trend of working from home is accelerating. The writing is on the wall for anyone who wants to read it:

"Jobs in corporate America are disappearing."
"The only security in life is self-reliance."

There are many angles you can take to attract more couples to your business.

✳   Start with the women already in your downline. They may be working maximum hours, which means they are not developing their business to its full potential. Bringing a partner in

134

to share the load could have a powerful effect on their future growth.

*   Many network marketers have talents that allow them to excel in certain areas while they struggle with others. Introducing a partner could be a shrewd business move. One plus one could equal three if the synergy is right.

*   One avenue to explore is couples without children where both work full-time. Supplementing their careers with a business could be a way to fast-track their way to financial independence. Keep an eye out for couples who talk about buying an investment property or flipping a house for profit. Ambitious, entrepreneurial couples will be open to exploring all avenues.

★ ★ ★ ★ ★ ★

Network marketing is an ideal third income stream. Couples who both work outside the home have a wide range of contacts. The business can be worked around career commitments.

*   Look for couples whose children have left home. A part-time network marketing business is a great way to fill the emotional void left by children who have scooted the coop. This is an ideal time to take stock of their finances and start bolstering that retirement fund.

*   Target couples in their forties and fifties. A network marketing business is great insurance against the loss of one or both incomes in the future.

Timing is important. I have spoken with many spouses eager to leave their jobs and join their partners in the business before the business is producing enough to replace their income. Often, the discussion takes place during the excitement of a convention or incentive trip. A record-breaking month or two can cause a rush to the head in a partner who is waiting for a chance to quit his or her day job and join in the fun of the business.

Network marketing is a volatile business. Stability doesn't

come until you personally develop several first-level leaders. A premature move from a single to a couple-driven enterprise could spell disaster for the business and the relationship. I advise couples to budget how much they need to live on, with a built-in buffer against weak months, before they commit. Once the plan is in place, they can start working toward it. Meanwhile, the best support a partner can offer may be to keep a regular income flowing into the household.

Spouses eager to be involved can make a big contribution on a part-time basis. There is never a shortage of tasks to check off. Even as simple a move as making a commitment to babysit more so their partners can schedule more parties could make a big difference to the business.

Can a married couple work together and stay married at the same time? If they want the partnership to be a happy as well as a profitable experience, establishing nine ground rules at the outset will help couples to avoid problems down the road:

1. Be clear about who does what. Don't waste time constantly looking over each other's shoulders.

2. Give each partner a share of creative and day-to-day responsibilities so both have maximum job satisfaction. Demoting one partner to the role of "dog's body" will lead to resentment.

3. Utilize each partner's strengths. If she is an organizer and he is a social person, there is a clear role for each to play. Let him do most of the communicating and training while she uses her management talents.

4. Try to find separate work spaces. Working together is fun, but it can also be distracting.

5. Talk often. Share ideas as well as enthusiasm.

6. Trust each other. You have the same goals and you share the rewards.

7. Don't flood the house with work-related stuff. Try not to bury family areas under piles of sales reports and invoices, but make an exception for promotions announcing fabulous trips and incentives—paste them everywhere!

8. Set boundaries. Making the business a 24/7 commitment will take the joy out of the experience. Maintaining separate phone lines for work and family is a good place to start.

9. Celebrate. One of the joys of working together is achieving together. Make the most of the good times.

A partnership that shares the work and the rewards with the person you care about most can be incredibly fulfilling. Open a new door to your opportunity and invite couples to enter it.

CHAPTER TWENTY-FOUR

Recruiting Close to Home

YOU DON'T HAVE TO LOOK FAR to find most of your prospects. They are among your current circle of friends, family, neighbors, and associates. They are people you already know!

How did you start your network marketing business? Probably you heard about it from a relative or friend. Now it's your turn to pay it forward.

The majority of newcomers join under someone in their inner circle. Don't let the fear of taking advantage of family and friends stop you from prospecting close to home. If you approach people sensitively, they won't cross the street to avoid you.

You made a list of everyone you knew when you started your business. If you haven't referred to it in a while, it's time to dust it off. If you were smart from the start, you will have kept adding to your list as you met new people. If you weren't, start now.

Relationships are what make this business work. You can spend a lifetime looking for people to build a relationship with, but you already have a relationship with the people around you. Why not prospect among the people who know you, like you, and trust you already? They may say no, but there is a chance they will say yes. Don't squander that chance.

You may have sold to friends and family when you started, but did you present the business? Even if you did, you now have more confidence, more experience, and more skills. The time may be ripe for a second approach.

There are protocols to follow when you are approaching people close to you. You'll know you've crossed the line if your phone stops ringing, your social invitations dry up, or the streets are deserted when you step out. Stay within the proper boundaries by adopting the following courtesies:

★ Never surprise your prospect. No one likes to be ambushed. Turn a social invitation into a business presentation and you deserve to be shown the door.

★ Call ahead before knocking on a friend's door.

★ Be upfront right from the start. Explain why you are calling and ask if the time is convenient before you launch into a presentation. Say, "This is a business call. Are you free to talk?"

★ Have a good reason for approaching any prospect, no matter how well you know him or her. You know your family and friends' circumstances, and your approach should reflect that.

★ Always offer your contact the escape route, such as "This business does not suit everyone, and only you can decide if it's for you."

★ Be generous with sincere compliments:

"I know my sponsor would be impressed by your experience/
   background."
"I'm approaching you because I have always admired you."

★ If you are new, ask people you know for their opinions. People love to be asked for help and advice. Work that to your advantage. Say, "I am excited about this business. What do you think?"

★ Ask friends if you can practice on them. Ask them to model your clothes, take your supplements, sample your chocolate, and try your skin care products. Samples work well for people you know, especially if you specify a time to follow up.

> "Use this cream every night this week and I'll call you Monday to see if you have noticed a difference."
> "Here is a fourteen-day supply of our supervitamin. Take one packet every morning and another at night. I guarantee you'll notice the difference. I'll follow up in two weeks to see if you agree."

★ Ask strategic questions to get family and friends thinking about joining you in the business, based around what you see in their homes.

> "What are you going to do with the photos you have stored in these boxes?"
> "Where did you buy these candles?"
> "Did you know you could get your vitamin supplements free?"
> "Have you ever thought about a different career?"
> "Ever thought about us working together? I think it would be amazing."

★ Give your products as birthday and Christmas gifts so family and friends can try them.

> "I can't wait to see what you think of our new catalog."
> "I immediately thought of you when I saw this season's colors."

★ You are in unique position with people you know. You know how they live, what their priorities are, and how they think. Try to preempt objections by saying, "The main reservation I had was [list a genuine one], but at training I learned . . ."

★ Focus on activities you can share, such as saying, "Imagine how much fun it would be to go on trips together. The next one is a week in the Caymans."

Don't discriminate against prospects because they're friends. If you are reluctant about prospecting close to home, apply the emotional test I talked about earlier. Imagine how you would feel if someone you knew signed with another company or under another representative. Ouch!

Do you know the golden rule of direct selling? It is "an opportunity is never lost. If you don't find it, someone else will."

Don't stop at family and friends when your immediate neighborhood beckons.

On a national average, one in ten of your neighbors is already running a home-based business. If this isn't the case in your neighborhood, even better—go door knocking.

Be yourself. If you are bright, enthusiastic, and warm, people will relate to you. Don't lose your nerve if people are rude. You wouldn't want them as customers or recruits anyway, and their curtness makes it easier to move on.

Make sure you haven't called at an inconvenient time. Say, "Hi. Thanks for coming to the door. I hope I haven't caught you at a bad time." Pause to give the person a chance to respond.

If you are nervous, say so. "This is the first time I have done this, so forgive me if I sound nervous." Who could refuse someone so forthright?

There is no magic script that I can give you, because the flow of the conversation will depend on the demeanor of the person opening the door. Try:

"We haven't met, but I'm Brittany. I live around the corner and I represent [. . .] in this area."

This is a good time to say something complimentary about the house, dog, child, car, or garden.

"I walk past your garden every day and always admire your roses."

"Is that your granddaughter? I wish my mom lived close to me."

"Your remodeling project looks amazing."

Your prospect's response will determine what happens from this point. The icebreaker is the tough part. Stick with the basic principles—ask questions and listen to what the prospect says. Don't deliver a prepared sales pitch. Here are some examples:

"Are you familiar with [. . .] products?"

"Do you have a local beauty/herb consultant?"

"Do you know about our home-shopping service?"

"May I quickly show you some of our most popular products?"

"Have you seen our educational toys for children your son's age?"

"Would you like a complimentary facial/makeover?"

Focus on a current reason for the visit.

"I'm calling because we have a special collection for spring [or Mother's Day, etc.]."

Consider holding an event you can invite neighbors to.

"I am calling to invite you to a preview of our holiday collection. Are you available on [date and time]? I would love for you to come."

I once worked with a distributor who sold beauty products in a small rural area. She made friends with the postman, who told her whenever a new family moved in. Within days, she stopped by to welcome the new family to the area. Almost always she picked up a new customer and sometimes she found a new recruit. No surprise that she was a top producer despite having a small base of people to work from.

Your next recruit could be sitting right under your nose. The only way to find out is to approach everyone you know and give that person the same chance someone offered you.

CHAPTER TWENTY - FIVE

Building a Part-Time Army

AS A PART-TIME BUSINESS, investing as little as five to ten hours a week can yield a significant income. Most network marketers work the business part-time. Millions of network marketers join solely to get their own products wholesale. Millions more join to service a few friends and family members.

Seven out of ten network marketers are small players, with the average network marketer working around five hours a week.

Is it worth building a part-time army of recruits? No question. You're paid on the total sales generated in your organization, so the more people you have the more you'll earn. And that's not all. Your next star could come into your business as a small player—loaded with tons of potential waiting to explode.

From college students and stay-at-home moms to full-time workers supplementing their wages and business owners promoting products that complement an existing business, there are many ways network marketing can work as a part-time job.

* The chance to start a new career without the expense of retraining

- ★ A diversion from a job that offers little stimulation or satisfaction
- ★ An alternative to working overtime
- ★ The tax advantages of running a business from home
- ★ Access to products they love at wholesale rates
- ★ The fun of learning new skills

It may be that your prospect would love to work from home, but leaving a full-time job prematurely can lead to unnecessary stress. The security of an existing job is an ideal way to start on the path toward full-time self-employment. Many network marketers begin with modest goals that expand once they see the potential of their network marketing business.

When you meet prospects who work full-time, ask if they have five hours a week for a part-time job. Motivated workers can find five hours a week and they're the ones we want. Party planners can fit one party a week, including booking, traveling, and hostess coaching into five hours. Even a modest profit of $100 at a party adds up to $5,000 a year.

There are 168 hours in every week. For most of us, time is not the issue. How we spend our time is the issue. No one got rich sitting on the couch watching *Seinfeld* reruns.

What you don't want is to set your prospects on a collision course with their employers. Suggest they follow these golden rules for combining two jobs:

- ★ As a courtesy, let your employer know you have started a small part-time business. Assure him or her it will not interfere with your work.

- ★ Never work your business on company time—not even an e-mail or phone call. Do an honest day's work for an honest day's pay.

- ★ Don't bombard your colleagues with your plans to quit.

Although they will be interested in your new business, unfavorable comments or comparisons about your full-time job will alienate them.

 ★ If you do bring your products or brochures to work, show them only during scheduled breaks.

 ★ Don't use company stationery. Not even a paper clip.

 ★ Do something to progress your business every day, no matter how small it is. Consistent effort will always win out over short bursts of activity. Plan the times you will work your business, and stick to them.

 ★ Don't let stress rob you of your enthusiasm and energy levels. If one person is stressed, the whole family suffers. Focus on the big picture and set a deadline. For example, you might tell yourself, "I will work at this pace for one year to build my business to the point when I can resign from my job."

 ★ Delegate household tasks to family members. If you share how your new business will benefit them all, they will be willing to pitch in. Offer an incentive such as an increased allowance to keep them motivated.

 ★ You are not Superman or Wonder Woman! Don't detract from the excitement of transitioning from working for someone else to working for yourself by taking on more than you can handle. Pay someone to do the cleaning, run errands, and mow the lawn. Money was meant to go around (and you may end up recruiting your hired help).

 ★ Save time by ordering direct and having your purchases delivered. Treat everyone who knocks on your door, including the guy who delivers your pizza and the mailman, as a prospect.

 ★ Concentrate on the core activities that will drive your business forward. Discard unnecessary distractions. Learn to say no to things you don't want to do. Put a timer near the phone to monitor the length of phone calls. Record your favorite programs so you can fast forward through the commercials.

Tell your part-time recruits it's not what you do, but how you do it that counts. They will earn the respect and admiration of family, friends, colleagues, and employers if they adopt the golden rules. Your part-timer could even end up recruiting his or her boss!

CHAPTER TWENTY-SIX

Prospect Shopping

THE SMARTEST WAY TO BUILD your organization is start with your inner circle of contacts and radiate out from that inner circle through bookings and referrals.

If you stray too far from the tried-and-true relationship-building formula, you send the wrong message to your recruits and distract them from the core business of booking, selling, and recruiting. However, there will be times when you need to build or restore momentum, such as the following instances:

* You decide to take your part-time business full-time.
* Your company introduces an incentive that will require an all-out effort.
* Your star performer is elevating in rank, so you must re-build your personal group.
* You need to regain lost ground after taking a break from your business.
* You hit a dry spell.

* You move to new town.

* You are mentoring people in your group who need help generating leads.

That is when it's time to go prospect shopping. Prospects are not going to come knocking on your door. You have to go out and find them—that is why it's called *prospecting*! If you actively look for prospects, you will find them everywhere you go. If you wait for them to jump in front of you, be prepared for a long wait.

Picture a desert and you will probably see only dry, barren landscape. It's hard to believe anything can survive such a harsh environment. But just beneath the dusty surface, millions of tiny seeds lie dormant. When it rains, the seeds seize the moment to germinate. Within days, the desert springs to life in glorious color.

It's the same with your business. In your hometown, there are hundreds, if not thousands, of people waiting for their chance to bloom. Perhaps they have big dreams but no idea how to achieve them. They may not have heard about your business or not understand what it's about. You can be the one who brings them to life.

The CEO of a major direct selling corporation once said; "We see ourselves as a personal-development business disguised as a business that sells products."

But who is going to know if you don't tell people?

When I first came to the United States, I knew no one. As a newcomer and an outsider, I had no choice but to meet people. As you can expect, no one returned my calls, answered my letters, or replied to my e-mails. It took months of dogged determination to make my first business contacts.

Was it tough? Absolutely.

Did I give up? Absolutely not. I believed I had something to offer and I was determined to be in the right place at the right time when the right people came along. I joined clubs and associations that catered to the direct selling industry. I subscribed to publications to identify the decision makers. I attended meetings to bring myself face-to-face with people. I submitted articles to get my name in front of possible clients.

My persistence paid off. I was given a small speaking spot at an industry event. It was a multiple-choice session with five or six speakers competing for the same audience. The room to which I was assigned was so far from the main event you practically had to take a bus to get there. Would people show up to hear a speaker they had never heard off?

I spent two days working the convention introducing myself to as many people as I could, and inviting them to come and hear me. But there were few sightings of the people I really wanted to target and I knew better than to approach tight-knit groups. My goal wasn't to annoy people.

Then a spark lit. I staked out the women's restroom and ta-dah! At the mirror, touching up her lipstick was one of the power players I had no chance of meeting in the main conference hall. I started a conversation, she agreed to come to hear me speak, and she honored her promise. A few weeks later she gave me my first booking. It takes a big dose of courage and a dash of chutzpah to build a business.

When it's time for you to go prospect shopping, you have a wealth of opportunities to meet potential recruits.

Take Advantage of Tools

From a simple opportunity brochure to CDs and DVDs that tell your story, tools help you get your message across. Find out what resources your corporation has. Was your business featured in a glossy magazine? Are your products featured in a newspaper? Magazines and newspapers help to establish credibility with their mix of articles, expert opinions, and personal success stories focusing on your products and opportunity.

Many corporations recommend you scatter them in your community, for example, in medical waiting rooms or restaurants, while others suggest you give them to existing customers, prospects, and party guests. Do them all, and include a note inside inviting the reader to contact you.

Tools are created for one reason. They make it easier to get the job done. They won't work if you're not using them. If you invest in say, ten magazines that feature your business, make sure they are always in circulation. Set a goal to give one out every day and to recycle them every ten days. Develop the habit of giving one out and retrieving one—every single day.

Increase Your Visibility in Your Community

If your goal is to meet more people, there is no shortage of ways to go about it. For example, try the following:

★ Join a club. From service clubs to social groups and business associations, your local community center or chamber of commerce will have an extensive list. Your local newspaper and community notice boards will be full of leads.

★ Teach or take an adult education class that will attract people who are likely to use your products—for example, cooking classes if you sell kitchen tools or food products.

★ Do you have an hour or two to spare? No one will decline your offer to volunteer at your local hospital, school, community center, or church. One good contact may be all it takes to enter a new circle.

★ Have your products delivered to your workplace to attract curious colleagues when you open the carton on your break. Make sure there is always a sample or relevant literature in your order so you can say, "Here, try (or read) this."

★ Talk to people in line at coffee shops, restrooms, bus stations, airports, shops, and supermarkets. Visit the library, go to garage sales, or chat to neighbors at your next tailgate party.

★   Turn casual encounters into contacts by asking, "What do you do?" When they ask you, say, "I have a great job—I'm a [company name] representative." At a store ask, "Do you enjoy working here?" When it's your turn, say, "I love my job. I sell spa products at home parties." At a restaurant, ask, "Have you eaten here before?" If the response warrants it, say, "I am a [company name] manager and my team meets here once a month." Or try, "I am celebrating, as I just won a free trip to Maui. Do you love to travel?"

★   Go to every event or social gathering to which you are invited. If you don't know a soul, try this technique to help you break the ice: Act like you're the host. You'll find it easier to mix and mingle.

★   Seize every opportunity to start a relationship. Relationship experts recommend these simple ways to kick-start a connection:

  ★   Do someone a favor.
  ★   Ask someone for help—for example, "I'm looking for . . ."
  ★   Offer your assistance—for example, "Do you need help?"
  ★   Loan something to someone.
  ★   Recommend something (book, website, etc.).
  ★   Give someone something.
  ★   Ask for advice/opinions.
  ★   Offer a compliment, such as "Nice tie!"

Promote Yourself

You will increase your chances of making contacts if you raise your profile in the community.

★ *Can you write?* Your local paper may be delighted to receive an article or opinion piece on a hot topic. You have everything to gain and nothing to lose. Send out press releases about new products, special events, and achievements. Before you send submissions, think about what will interest readers of that publication. Call ahead to check editorial policy and submit your contribution as professional writers do—that is, double-spaced on good quality paper, with spelling and grammar checked. Make sure the content is topical. Old news or tired arguments rarely make it to print. An interesting photo will increase your chances of publication.

★ *Do you enjoy speaking?* Community, professional, business, charitable, and social groups always need speakers to fill their programs. A twenty- to thirty-minute presentation that is entertaining and informative will win over most audiences. Some groups will welcome demonstrations on scrapbooking, mix-and-match wardrobe planning, chocolate making, preparing nutritional/gourmet meals in minutes, or decorating your home for the upcoming season. Tailor your speech to your audience and use your imagination to come up with catchy title for the organizers to circulate. Some ideas are:

Are legal drugs (the foods we eat) killing us?
Seven sins that accelerate skin aging
Can chocolate be good for you?
Create ten looks from five simple pieces for summer
Make your own candles
Jump-start your kids' education
How I turned a hobby into a business

You are more likely to be invited back or referred to other clubs if you entertain and inform.

Don't restrict yourself to your products. What about a speech on:

The tax breaks of working from home
How I funded my retirement in five hours a week

In return for valuable advice and insights everyone can take away, you get to promote your business to a captive audience.

✴ *Does your community have a local newspaper?* Take advantage of topics making news (such as rising obesity levels) by writing to the editor of your local rag. Clip and copy or scan your letter to send with your next customer newsletter.

Promote Your Business

Make it easy for people to know that you have a business opportunity.

✴ Rent a booth at the mall or at a trade show, church bazaar, or school fair. If the cost is prohibitive, make it a team effort. Make sure your booth is more eye-catching than your competitors' booths. Free samples, tasting stations, giveaways, lucky draws, demonstrations, and on-the-spot consultations are crowd pullers. Balloons and lollipops will attract kids, and their parents will be close behind.

✴ Create your own mini expo. Set a theme, such as "Start a business from home" or "Celebrate the holidays in style" or "Fabulous foods in minutes." Invite other network marketers and suppliers to participate. It's no accident that businesses such as car dealerships, antique shops, cafés, and restaurants congregate in one area. It increases foot traffic. The bigger the event, the more likely your local paper will cover it when you ask.

✴ Display a notice on your local community board with a simple message, such as:

Free seminar on starting a home-based business!
Free style consultation!

Part-time salespeople needed!
Summer jobs for students!

✶ Hold an event in an area with plenty of foot traffic. Walk around the block handing out invitations to people on the sidewalk. Bribe friends and family to help if you need more foot soldiers.

✶ Hand out vouchers—for example, for a mini-facial. Make them sound special: "I have ten of these to give out and I would love you to have one," or "I have just met my sales target for the month and have five free facials cards to give out."

✶ Send out a promotional mailer. Direct mail experts say only half the recipients of a mailer promoting a special offer will open it. Here is a checklist to increase your chances of a prospect reading and responding to your offer:

1. Make sure it has instant eye appeal. A novel shape, size, or color will help to make it stand out.
2. Offer a generous coupon-only discount or a "buy one, get one free" offer.
3. Stick to one message.
4. Check that your contact details are included.
5. Before you dispatch any promotion, check, check, and check again for errors.

✶ Postcards cost less to send than letters, and they do not have to be opened so your offer will jump off the page. Send postcards to announce new releases, specials, or incentives. For example, suppose your company releases the qualification for a trip to Mexico and it includes a first-timer's qualification. A postcard announcing, "Can you sell? In the next six months, you could win a free trip to Mexico. Call now for details," is sure to strike a chord with some of the recipients.

✶ Sponsor a sports team, charity run, or tournament. Make

sure your banner, advertisement, or flyers are prominently displayed, and offer to present the prizes.

★ Try this job satisfaction survey in a mall or on the street (asking permission first). Invite people to answer yes or no to the following questions, comparing their "ideal" to their "current" job:

____ I set my own schedule.

____ I am recognized when I perform well.

____ My company pays for my annual vacation.

____ I can take my vacations when it suits me.

____ I choose how much I earn.

____ I receive ongoing training.

____ I receive monthly performance bonuses.

____ I can earn a company car.

____ I take time off to attend to personal or family matters.

____ I can take advantage of tax breaks.

If there are too many mismatches between your current and ideal job, it may be time to consider to a network marketing business.

There are promotional opportunities in abundance if you go looking for them. They all work, but you have to choose which will work best for you. Whatever you choose, do it with style and flair. Whether it's a speech, an article, a booth, or a mail drop, it is going to be your store window. Ill-prepared or ill-presented promotions won't help you or your business.

Above all, make sure prospect shopping does not interfere with your day-to-day business. Even if your efforts are successful, if you neglect your existing customers and recruits, you may find you have taken one step forward and two steps backward.

CHAPTER TWENTY - SEVEN

How to Get Referrals

THE THREE MAGIC WORDS in party plan or network marketing are: "Bring a friend."

Your next superstar is just as likely to come from your "accidental" prospect as the person you have been targeting for months. You know who is right for your business, and the friend who attends your event in a support role could turn out to be a perfect fit. You'll never know if you don't have a chance to meet the person.

Whatever event you're planning—celebration, training, meeting, product preview, opportunity night, or business seminar—asking every guest to bring a friend will dramatically increase your contacts. If your husband or partner can't make it to a convention and your corporate policy allows it—bring a friend. Who could resist the color, excitement, and energy of an annual convention?

If you are a party planner, include "bring a friend, get a gift" reminders with every invitation. If your invitations are preprinted, invest in a set of vivid "Bring a friend, get a gift" labels and affix them to the envelope. Ask hostesses to invite every guest to bring a friend, and add the incentive of a free gift to everyone who does. Don't leave it to chance. Give your hostess a target and offer a bonus gift if she achieves it.

To add to the personal referrals generated through your "bring a friend" program, there are many ways to conjure up new contacts.

★   At parties and opportunity events, play a referrals game. Hand out a blank sheet of paper and ask guests to write down the names of anyone whom they think may be interested in hosting or attending a similar event. Set the timer to three minutes to generate a little competitive excitement. The guest with the most names wins, you get the leads, and the winner has also identified herself to you as a natural networker. Prospect alert!

★   The simplest way to generate referrals is to ask for them. Increase your success rate by making specific suggestions to help your contact think of names.

"Can you think of anyone who would be good at what I do?"
"Who is the most enthusiastic/hardworking person you know?"
"Do you know anyone who . . .
    . . . has been in direct selling before?"
    . . . talks about having his or her own business?"
    . . . is looking for part-time work?"
    . . . wears a lot of jewelry?"
    . . . has fabulous skin?"
    . . . is interested in herbs/essential oils?"
    . . . works at a health club or fitness center?"
    . . . recently sold or is trying to sell a business?"
    . . . has lots of friends?"

Follow by asking, "What do you like/admire most about him or her?" You'll get a warm response if you can say, "Nikki gave me your name. She says you have more friends than anyone she knows." Or, "Matt says you are the hardest-working person he knows."

It is a good idea to ask anyone who gives you referrals to call ahead and let those people know you will be calling. It's even better if the person agrees to give a reason and why he thinks the referee may be interested in your call.

★   Keep a supply of "$10 or 10 percent off your next purchase" vouchers on hand ready to reward and encourage people to pass along leads.

★   If you deliver, pop an incentive for referrals into customer orders.

★   Add a referral byline that offers an incentive to respond to every e-mail, newsletter, and communication you send out.

★   A few successful network marketers I know purchase lists of qualified leads. I am still deliberating this one. I used to advise against them but have noticed the lists are improving all the time, so I may reverse my decision. In the meantime, I'll let you be the judge.

★   Referrals do not need to come from existing contacts. You can create referrals by approaching businesses that target your market and asking to leave brochures and newspapers. Think Pilates, yoga, and exercise classes for health products; private kindergartens and daycare centers for toys; veterinarian clinics for pet products. Sweeten the deal with free products if necessary. With a little imagination, you can create a win-win situation. In exchange for displaying your material, offer vouchers the business can use to attract new people through its doors.

There is only one way you will fail to get referrals and that is not to ask for them. Develop a referrals mind-set and you will get your leads.

PART III

Turning Knowledge into Practice

CHAPTER TWENTY-EIGHT

The Dress Rehearsal

THINK OF THE WORLD AS YOUR STAGE, so you don't perform unrehearsed. Before you start calling your prospects, work on your lines and how you will deliver them.

Most of us think visually, so we translate the words we hear into pictures. We "see" the characters in the books we read, and we dream in color. When you make a business presentation, you create word-pictures of the business for your prospect. The more vivid they are, the more likely it is you will inspire the prospect to act.

Before you step into the spotlight, check that the message you want to convey is reflected in your words.

Simple or Easy?

This business is simple. It's not easy. It takes time and energy to build a network marketing business. If you create the impression that it will be easy, you set your prospects up for frustration and disappointment. Create a realistic picture of the commitment involved and you are less likely to waste time training and mentoring people who lack the desire, the drive, or the skills to succeed.

Earn or Make?

Although the commissions and bonuses paid on your sales may appear to be high on paper, you earn what you deserve. In most jobs, you are paid for showing up. Employers base their wage budgets on both productive and nonproductive time. They factor in vacation and sick days, health benefits, and 401(k) contributions. They cover times when business is slow or employees are slack.

Network marketing pays for results. You only get paid when products are sold, and you have to work hard to build a profitable business. Avoid the phrase "make money" and use the more accurate "earn money" instead.

Offer or Ask?

Why do some people find it hard to recruit? Mostly, it's because they lack the confidence to ask!

Pretend you are sitting in front of a large cake. It's luscious dark chocolate with rich velvety frosting. Across the table, another person is eyeing the cake. Compare these two scenes:

1. The cake belongs to the person sitting across from you. You would die for a slice, but you're too shy, polite, or embarrassed to ask. What if the person says no? You forgo your chance to enjoy the cake.

2. The cake is yours. There's plenty to share, and you are delighted to offer a slice to the person sitting across from you. How do you feel? Kind? Generous? Absolutely. You

have given someone else the opportunity to share your enjoyment. Same people, same cake, different perspectives.

It's no different with network marketing. You are offering prospects an opportunity to learn about your business and to help them get started if they decide to proceed. You are not trying to coerce or convince them. Be generous in sharing your opportunity with as many people as possible, and let them decide if they want to accept.

Underpromise or Underdeliver?

It's hard to hold back when you're brimming with enthusiasm. But step carefully. The benefits of a network marketing or party plan business don't need to be exaggerated. It's better to surprise and delight your recruits when their expectations are exceeded than to have a disillusioned recruit on your hands.

Details or Highlights?

Details do not sell the business. If movie producers revealed the full plot in the promotional blurb, you'd pass on the show. Do what the producers do. Focus on enticing highlights.

Make sure you can answer these questions in thirty seconds or less:

"What's unique about your products?"
"What's special about your opportunity?"
"How do I get started?"
"What help will I get?"
"How do I find customers?"
"How do I find recruits?"
"How much does it cost to start?"

"Are there other costs involved?"

"How do I get paid?"

"What makes you think I could do this?"

Make your words sound conversational, not like you are delivering lines from a script. Get to the point. If you are being long-winded, delete unnecessary or ambiguous information. Practice with a stopwatch until you have mastered the thirty-second sound bite.

Here is an example that demonstrates how to present a compensation plan in thirty seconds.

> "The plan outlines what you'll earn. You start at 30 percent on personal sales and 3 percent on the sales of anyone you recruit. When you move up to manager, you earn up to 50 percent on your personal sales and 10 percent on your team. It's pretty amazing. The more you do, the more you earn. Whether you want to earn $100 a week or $10,000 a month is up to you."

Before you say another word, ask a question based on your prospect's reaction.

"Does that make sense?"

"What do you think?"

"Any questions?"

When your prospect asks a question or makes a comment, take it as permission to speak for another thirty seconds on the area that interests the person or to clarify a point the person doesn't understand. You enhance your chance of an attentive audience when you respond to their questions rather than taking it upon yourself to decide what they want to hear.

Run through this final checklist of the common mistakes made by inexperienced and overeager business builders. If you suspect these mistakes apply to you, they probably do. Fix them before you blow your chances of making a great impression on every prospect, every time.

   ★ *Too Much Information!* No one cares when the company started or the exact percentage paid on every level of your compensation plan.
   Fix it: Decide "What is the one thing my prospect needs to know to move to the next step?" and stay in that zone.
   ★ *Boring Your Prospect.* Fix it: Bringing your presentation to life with colorful anecdotes, interesting examples, and questions. You have a limited amount of time to make your point. Don't waste it!
   ★ *Exaggerating Your Competitive Advantage.* Don't make exaggerated claims, such as, "We are the fastest growing, we pay the most . . ."
   Fix it: Without access to other companies' data, can you be sure of your facts? If not, zip it. Your time is better spent focusing on your prospects' needs.
   ★ *Overemphasizing Money!* Fix it: People join this business for a myriad of reasons. Share more than the financial benefits, or you will lose prospects looking for a fresh challenge, the chance to meet new people, learn new skills, and have fun.
   ★ *Too Much "I" Speak.* Fix it: This is not about you. It is about your prospect. Talk about him and he will stay tuned to what you are saying.

   Don't leave success to chance. You wouldn't step out onto a stage without several rehearsals. The better prepared you are and the more empathy you have with the people you are performing for, the greater your chance of being a sensation.

CHAPTER TWENTY-NINE

Approaching Your Prospects

THE MORE PEOPLE YOU APPROACH, the more appointments you will make. The more appointments you hold, the more people you will recruit. The sooner you start, the sooner you will get results. You have to fall in love with the phone.

If you truly want to be a recruiting superstar—why settle for less?—you'll need to develop a ten-call-a-day habit. Not only will you relax once you warm up a little, but you increase your chances of a yes answer with every call.

Pick an hour that fits your schedule, and turn it into your daily power hour. The only calls to make in your power hour are these prospecting calls:

* Calls to new prospects
* Follow-up calls to ongoing prospects
* Calls to referrals
* Cold calls to create a prospect

These tips will help you make the most of every call:

✴   Before you pick up the phone, take a few deep breaths to relax your voice. Focus on breathing out, as deeply as you can, then refill your lungs and push that air out again.

✴   Make sure you are sitting away from the hubbub of television and family noise. Close the door to avoid interruptions.

✴   Challenge yourself to stay in the room until the hour is up. No sneaky coffee refills or checking on laundry in the drier allowed. Distractions are not your friend.

✴   If you are calling someone you know, take time for a few minutes of small talk.

✴   Adopt a conversational, enthusiastic tone, as if you were calling to recommend a must-see movie.

✴   Keep the call short. You erase the reason for the appointment if you share everything on the phone.

✴   Don't read or follow a script. Be sincere and be yourself.

✴   Ask questions and listen to what your prospect is saying. Aim for a two-way conversation rather than a business pitch.

✴   Don't take a "no" personally. This is a business call, not a personal call, and any rejections relate to your business not to you.

✴   Whatever the outcome, say, "Thank you for your time, it was good to talk with you." Pop a note with a discount voucher in the mail. The gesture will be appreciated and make it easy for you to call again.

✴   Review each call. What went well? What didn't? Adjust before you pick up the phone for the next call. Practice makes perfect. Try different approaches until you find one that works. Above all, don't take yourself too seriously. A sense of humor is a great asset at the front line, and if you're not having fun, where's the point?

✴   Voice mails don't count and neither do calls to your mom.

Try to make ten business calls in your power hour, even if it means going overtime.

The flow of your calls will depend on the relationship you have with your prospect as well as on your own personality.

★　★　★　★　★　★

Here are some suggestions you can mix, match, and adapt.

Start every call by introducing yourself and asking, "Do you have a few minutes?" or "Is this a good time to talk?"

If the answer is, "This isn't a good time," or "I'm just about to go out," ask, "Is tomorrow morning okay?" or "Is the weekend better?"

If the answer is yes, continue with, "I'm so pleased I caught you at a good time. Let me tell you why I'm calling."

I like the following openers because they are direct and show a little chutzpah:

"I'm calling to ask you to come and work with me."
"I'm calling to invite you to join our team."
"I'm calling to offer you a job."

Make sure you are ready with the magic word, "Because . . ." If you don't have a "because," don't make the call. Try the following approach for someone whose background indicates a great match for your business:

You: "Ray, did you know some of the most successful people in our industry are [artists/teachers/engineers]?"
Ray: "Why is that?"

Personalize your explanation. If Ray is a teacher, say: "I'm sure it's because you are such great communicators."

You can add as much as you like: "Being a teacher gives you immediate credibility."

When you are new, try the following approach with people you know:

You: "Hi, Jan. It's Ruby. Guess what? I've started my own business!"

Because Jan knows you well, she will ask, "What business?"

You reply: "I'm selling the most amazing range of [beauty/health/educational] products. I have just finished training, and I'd love you to be one of the first I show the products to, because [you always look amazing/I always respect your opinion/you know what it's like to have your own business]. I can't wait to get your take on them. Are you free one night this week? It will only take an hour."

For a ground-floor opportunity, try saying:

"Someone is going to tell you about this and I want to be the first."

To call a good customer, try:

You: "I have been meaning to call you for ages and have decided not to put it off any longer."

Izak: "What is it?"

You: "I want to talk to you about the business."

Izak: "What about it?"

You: "You are exactly the sort of person we are looking for. You clearly love the products and . . ."

For a top prospect, follow these lines:

"At training, I was asked who would be the first person I would approach and I immediately thought of you."

"As soon as I decided to do this, I thought about who I would most like to work with, and it was you."

To invite your friends to a business launch party, try:

"Hi Beki. Remember I mentioned I was starting my own (company name) business?

Well, it's going even better than I hoped. So much so, I'm having a few friends over to celebrate. I hope you can come. Are you free Tuesday next week?"

Be sure to make your celebration special. Create a festive atmosphere, be generous with samples, and focus on your friends rather than delivering a long spiel about your business. Show some products and give every guest a hostess pack. At the end of the party, say: "I can't wait to do a party for you, because look what you get as a hostess."

To call a friend you have not yet contacted, try:

You: "Hi, Frances. I have been meaning to call you for weeks, so this morning I put you at the top of my list. How are things with you?"

After catching up with her news, say: "I have finally done something I have been thinking about for a while. I've started my own business."

Frances: "What are you doing?"

You: "I went to a [company name] party and had such a great time I decided to become a consultant myself. I thought you may be interested because . . ."

To approach someone who has expressed disappointment with a previous network marketing experience, try:

"Hello James, it's Brad. I'm Mark's neighbor and he gave me your number. He mentioned you briefly had a network marketing business."

Depending on James' reaction, you might say: "I started with another company too and only stayed three months. For a

while I thought I wouldn't do it again, but when I was introduced to [company name], things were different."

Explain what changed your mind.

"I get so much more support."
"The products are much easier to sell."
"The compensation plan is simpler."

Your response will depend on the feedback you get, but make
sure it includes: "Because I'd been in network marketing before,
I knew what I was looking for."

To call someone you met through a third party, try:

"Kaydence, this is Tiffany calling. We met at Anna's graduation.
Remember I mentioned I have my own business selling
[nutrition/education/beauty] products? Well, I'm expanding
my business and you are exactly the sort of person I am
looking for. You are such fun to be around."

Take the pressure out of the call by asking:

"Are you free one afternoon for coffee so I can show you what
it's about? Then you can decide if you want to take it further."

If you make your prospects feel special, give them specific
reasons why you believe they have what it takes, and make it
clear you are not going to pressure them, you will get your appointments. The more often you pick up the phone, the sooner
you will build your organization.

CHAPTER THIRTY

The Recruiting Interview

IF THERE IS A MAGIC MOMENT in network marketing, it's when you are about to present the business to your prospects. If you have brought them to this point, you must be playing your cards right. You have every reason to feel confident and in control.

No matter how excited you are, try to relax. You will repeat this process many times and you cannot predict who will accept and who will not. Your prospects will come from different backgrounds and have different experiences and perceptions. They will filter everything you say through their own beliefs and prejudices. You can control the quality of your message, but you cannot control your prospect's decision.

When you are ready to start the interview, the following steps will increase your chances of hearing the four words you want to hear: "Where do I sign?"

 ＊ Thank your prospect for meeting with you and tell the person you will take no more than forty minutes of his or her time. The person may be thinking, "I can't wait to start my own business and I can't think of anyone better to sign with." Lucky you. Unless you make a cat's breakfast of the interview, you're about to sign a new recruit. The person could also be thinking, "Why did I get myself into this?" or "What excuse can I give?"

Give the prospect time to relax, get to know you, and be reassured he or she is not about to be ambushed. Thank the person for coming, explain why you approached him or her—because you think he or she has what it takes—and you're here to help the prospect decide if the business has something to offer him or her. Feel the tension easing?

★ Invite your prospects to talk about themselves. We all love talking about ourselves and we love people who give us the opportunity to do so.

★ Ask lots of questions. The better your questions, the better the information you will receive. Genuine listeners always find the right questions because the conversation leads naturally to the next step. Without sounding like a drill sergeant, try to find out what you can about your prospect's career/financial hot buttons.

"How long have you worked in your current job?"
"What do you like most about it?"
"Is there anything you don't like?"
"What does your ideal job look like?"
"What is your dream annual income?"
"What would you do differently if you earned that much?"
"What are your long-term financial goals?"

Before you ask any question, think, "What am I trying to learn?" The point of a question is to understand the other person's viewpoint, not to labor your own or to put words in his or her mouth. Give people as much time as they need to answer. Hold your tongue until they have finished talking. This doesn't mean when they pause to draw breath, but when they are truly finished. If you talk too soon, you will miss the gems.

✳ When you feel the time is right, say, "Let me give you an overview of how the business works." Avoid quoting from the corporate manual. Keep the focus strictly on the person sitting across the table from you, tailoring your presentation to his or her circumstances, ambitions, and current priorities.

✳ Explain your business in simple terms with no industry jargon. Words like *upline, downline, width,* or *depth* and abbreviations like IBO, PV, and BV could confuse or alienate your prospects. If you are introducing concepts that may be new to them, check as you go, asking, "Does this make sense?" or "Am I explaining this well enough?"

✳ Keep your enthusiasm in check. Make sure you are not lapsing into a one-sided business pitch. Stop frequently to invite questions. Your confident, relaxed demeanor will impress your prospect.

✳ Don't panic when you get an objection. Objections are an invitation to share more information. Remind your prospects you are not trying to convince or persuade them. You want them to make the best decision for themselves. You will find suggested answers to common objections in Chapter Thirty-Two.

✳ Ask, "What do you think?" and wait for the answer so prospects can make their decision without interruption. There can be a fine line between a yes and a no. Applying pressure will diminish your chances of hearing, "Where do I sign?"

✳ If there are no questions and time is on your side, say, "The most common question I get asked is . . ." or "The biggest question I had before I joined was . . ."

✳ If your prospect is hooked, sign the agreement on the spot and confirm starter kit and training details. If prospects are unsure, you have several options to keep them alive:

     ✳ Invite the prospect to an upcoming event.

     ✳ Offer to meet again once the prospect has thought

about your proposal, perhaps involving his or her
partner next time.

* Lend prospects a CD or DVD that will help them
  learn more about the business.

* Lend them a magazine that features your company,
  referring them specifically to articles that match their
  circumstances. "You should check out the article on
  page 46. It's about one of our top people and she so
  reminds me of you. She was a working mom too, before she joined."

* Invite them to listen to a live or recorded call that
  outlines the business.

* Recruiting superstars never give the impression they are
trying to force a decision. A great way to keep your prospect hot,
but not feeling pressured, is to say, "Put our discussion today to
the back of your mind. You'll know this is for you if you find
yourself thinking about it a lot, or our conversation keeps popping into your head. That's a sign you should give it a try."

* Whatever the outcome, thank the person for meeting
with you and try to leave the door open. Most direct sellers admit
to being approached two to three times before they signed. Carry
a few "no" packs with you—free samples, special offers, discount
vouchers, even front-row invitations to upcoming product
launches—anything else that encourages the person to stay in
touch. Don't waste a great opportunity to build a strong relationship with good prospects just because the timing wasn't right.

The more appointments you have, the closer you are to finding the quality recruits you are looking for. There is only one
guaranteed way to fail in this business and that's not to ask.

CHAPTER THIRTY-ONE

The Business Seminar

THERE ARE THREE TYPES OF BUSINESS SEMINARS or opportunity nights: the good, the bad, and the ugly.

The good ones are geared toward guests. The bad ones focus on the company and the products. The ugly ones focus on the presenters. Save the celebrations and self-congratulations for an insider event. If your goal is to attract new representatives, gear every part of your program to them.

The following steps will ensure you make the most of your business seminar.

Step One

Start at the beginning—attracting a full house!

The more prospects you invite, the more will come. The more people in the room, the more electricity you will generate and the greater your chances of a storm of new sign-ups.

Distribute invitations with date, time, venue, and RSVP details. Personal invitations with an RSVP work better than open invitations. Include a few highlights of the event as well as any door prizes or giveaways you have planned. Add an element of excitement by numbering all invitations. Guests simply add their contact details and bring the invitation along to enter a lucky prize draw (and you get your up-to-date guest list).

Get your downline recruits working with you to fill the room. Challenge them to invite at least one guest from each of the following categories—customers, hostesses, neighbors, relatives, friends, coworkers, or someone who declined their offers before.

The better your guests know the person extending the invitation, the more likely they are to show. That is why you keep in touch with everyone on your hot and warm lists. A well-run business seminar may impress them enough to tip the scales in your favor.

Keep promoting the event. The more you promote it, the more likely your people will think of guests to invite. You may even like to run an incentive that rewards the recruit who brings the most qualified guests.

Follow every invitation with a call. The two reasons confirmed guests don't show is:

1. They forget.
2. They make a last-minute decision that they can't be bothered.

Personal calls will reduce your no-shows. Explain that you appreciate knowing if they cannot attend so you can invite someone else.

There is nothing like the echo of an empty room to dampen an event, so if you are short on numbers, co-opt a few friends to help create a lively atmosphere. The best guarantee of a full house is a track record of great events. Your people will want to bring guests if they know it will be a lively, fun night.

Step Two

Preparation makes perfect.

Map out a program that includes a variety of speakers who are most likely to connect with the audience. Any longer than sixty minutes of formal presentation and thirty minutes of informal mingling and your guests will bolt for the door the first chance they get.

Choose a master of ceremonies who is entertaining, efficient, and can create empathy with the audience. A good MC will know how to make guests feel relaxed and included.

Organize a simple display of the starter kit and your best-selling products so guests can look, touch, and smell.

Make sure your audiovisuals are in good shape. Nothing spells amateur like a sound system or PowerPoint meltdown.

Involve everyone in your organization in the event. You need support crew before and during the event, as well as greeters and presenters.

Fit the room to the audience. Put out only enough chairs for expected guests and keep a few spare ones to bring in at the last minute if numbers exceed expectations. Strategically placed plants and displays can make a large space feel more intimate if numbers fall short.

Have a dress rehearsal to iron out any problems. An ill-prepared speaker can destroy all your careful preparation in an instant. Inexperienced speakers often misjudge their timing. What may feel like five minutes at the microphone could easily stretch to fifteen, and there goes your program.

Step Three

Create an upbeat atmosphere from the start.

You want guests to feel welcome. That includes clear signage outside the venue so that no one gets lost. Ample parking and good lighting are basic courtesies. If you have issues with parking or the position of the room you are using, position helpers in strategic places to direct vehicle and foot traffic.

Music will help lift the atmosphere of the room, as will greeters at the door and name tags. Hand all guests information on the business and a program that includes the time the meeting will finish. If your product lends itself to sampling, offer samples at the start.

Step Four

Start and finish on time—no exceptions!

Don't allow latecomers to steal time from those who took the trouble to arrive on time. Position a greeter at the door to quietly usher latecomers into the back row you have left vacant for that purpose.

The MC should start by thanking guests for coming and create the mood by saying they are in for a great night.

Keep the formal part of the presentation short and dynamic. You are selling the sizzle, so save the details for training. If you don't want guests nodding off, let no speaker have the microphone for more than five minutes maximum. Make sure every speaker has a specific topic and that each one sticks to it.

"Our products sell because . . ."

"The business changed my life because . . ."

The more speakers on the program, the more chance you have to keep your guests' attention. Every speaker will connect with different guests, especially if they address different angles of the business. If one works the business full-time, make sure the next speaker combines the business with a regular job. If one speaker does not have children, the next should be working the business around family.

When they speak from the heart, they will touch hearts.

"I always wanted to own my own business, but I never did any- thing about it. I guess I was nervous it wouldn't work out. So for years, I stayed in an accounting/engineering job I didn't enjoy, working for a boss I didn't like. Then, I met my sponsor and he inspired me to follow my dreams. That was a year ago, and my only regret is I didn't have the courage to do it sooner."

Never assume guests understand how the business works. Briefly cover the corporate/distributor relationship.

"We have a great relationship with the company. They take care of the back end of the business so that we can focus on marketing the products and helping people like you start your own business. It's the perfect partnership. Our earnings plan works like this . . ."

All speakers should watch for audience reactions to what they are saying. They will know if they are becoming long-winded by the glazed eyes, restless body language, stifled yawns, or worse—people leaving. That means it is time to change the pace or exit stage left.

Discreet timing lights or signals will ensure no one overruns his or her allotted time. A good MC will not be afraid to signal a speaker who is misreading the audience to pick up the pace or to wind up the segment. If there's a hiccup, adjust the program to bring it back on track.

If you have a short, interesting DVD, play it. If it is full of pictures of the founders or home office, play it after your guests have safely left the room. Buildings and photos of founders do not sell the business. People who build relationships build businesses.

Step Five

Finish with a call to action.

At the end of the presentation invite guests to join, directly and sincerely. You won't get what you don't ask for. A "do it now" offer will help prompt a decision on the spot.

Be positive as if you expect guests to join. Hand out agreements and pens and talk through the steps to get started, focusing on the value that comes with the starter kit. Explain how to pay and say, "If there is any particular point you are stuck on, fill out the rest and leave that one blank. We'll have time to talk about it at the end of the program."

Point to the starter kit and invite guests to look at it after the presentation. Make sure everyone is clear about what the next step is, for example, attending the first training session on Saturday of the following week. Thank everyone for coming and draw the lucky door prize, which you have left to the end to encourage guests to stay.

Step Six

Give guests a reason to linger.

Simple refreshments will encourage guests to stick around and ask questions they may not have been brave enough to bring up in front of the group. This is not the time to be chatting to fellow organizers or friends who have come along to support your event.

Every guest should be assigned to one of your recruits to ensure no guest is left unattended. Adapt the closing statements I have covered in previous chapters, and especially in Chapters Eight and Nine, to suit to encourage hesitators to act.

Step Seven

Follow up with all guests within twenty-four hours.

Thank guests for coming, and ask if they have questions. Think of the business seminar as the start of the relationship, not a one-off chance to sign a few recruits.

A well-planned, well-executed business seminar is an excellent way to showcase your opportunity. Do it well and you will be rewarded with a surge of new recruits and contacts.

CHAPTER THIRTY-TWO

Loving Objections

YOU SHOULD LOOK FORWARD to questions and objections. They reveal what your prospects are thinking, such as:

*   They are interested.
*   They are testing you.
*   They have legitimate concerns that need to be addressed.
*   They are thinking of an excuse to say no.
*   They want to clarify a point.
*   They want more information.
*   They are seriously considering your opportunity.

When you are confident and enthusiastic about your business, you will see objections as an invitation to talk more about your opportunity.

Assume every question is a genuine attempt to find answers. Some objections are leading up to a "no," but you have to sort through them to find the "yes." This is no different from any job situation where many applicants are interviewed before the right candidate is found.

If your prospect says yes with unresolved issues hanging in the air, he or she has less chance of succeeding. And guess who the prospect will blame? The point of the interview is to find a fit between your prospect and your business. If there isn't a fit, don't force it.

Here is a range of responses to objections you can mix and match to fit most situations.

★ My standard response to objections is to agree with them. Arguing with or overriding an objection is a put-down. Agreeing shows respect for your prospect's perspective and concerns.

> Emma: "I don't see myself as a salesperson."
> You: "I agree. You don't come across that way. That's why I approached you. You seem so genuine and we're looking for people like you, not high-pressure salespeople."
> "You have such a bubbly personality—people will warm to you."

★ A popular response is to say, "I know how you feel." Your prospects will relax when you show empathy.

> Adam: "I'm not sure I can sell."
> You: "I know how you feel. I had never been in sales before and I wasn't sure it was for me. But I got over my reluctance once I saw how people loved the products."

★ An objection can trigger a conversation that leads to the discovery of a hot button.

> Gary: "I'm pretty happy with my job."
> You: "What do you do?"
> Gary: "I'm an engineer."
> You: "My cousin's an engineer. He loves it. Who do you work for?"

Gary: "I work for the city."

You: "Did you know some of the most successful people in this business are engineers? I have one who works the business part-time for the variety and the free vacation."

Gary: "You get a free vacation? Half the time I don't even take my vacation."

★　An objection could be a shield to fend off a high-pressure pitch. If you adopt a conversational tone, your prospect will relax.

Kelly: "I'm too busy."

You: "With two kids and a part-time job, you must be incredibly busy. I know how it feels. I was working full-time [or both my kids were under five, or . . .] when I started. Luckily for me, my sponsor was incredible. She helped me sort my schedule so I could do two parties a week. Starting small is fine. The extra money has made a huge difference to us."

This is a good time to explain any time-saving innovations your company has introduced. For example, if your company sends out personalized newsletters on your behalf, let your customer know how much time that saves and the sales it generates with little effort on your part. Talk about direct shipping and/or the wholesale buying program.

Someone with babysitting problems will be interested if training is available on DVD and through teleseminars and conference calls.

★　Some objections enable you to test your prospect's commitment.

Sarah: "I don't have the money."

You: "I understand. There are a couple of ways we can handle this."

Test her sincerity and initiative by suggesting ways to earn the starter kit.

★ Hosting one or two parties, with the proceeds going toward the kit

★ Using the catalog to gather orders from family and friends

★ Saving the money from the housekeeping budget over a few weeks

★ Holding a garage or yard sale to raise cash

★ Asking family members who give birthday or Christmas gifts to contribute toward the kit

★ Taking a job for a few weeks to raise the money

If genuine intent exists, your prospects will find a way to pay for the kit. If they don't have the money, the contacts, or the energy, you may be better off without them. Never make the mistake of offering to fund your prospect. In my experience, if prospects can't find the money for the kit, they rarely succeed. The behavior and attitudes that caused their financial woes in the first place will still be there after they sign. The most accurate indicator of future behavior is past behavior.

★ Don't be taken off guard by personal questions.

Angela: "How much money do you make?"

Answer truthfully, including how you made the money and what your goals are. What your prospect is really thinking is: "How much will I make?"

You: "I sell about $[. . .] a month to make sure I reach the[. . .] percent commission level on my personal sales, and I earn [. . .] percent on the sales of my group."

"I average ten appointments a week and my average sale is $[. . .]. So I am already making $[. . .] a week. Plus, I now have [. . .] people in my organization. My goal is to be earning $[. . .] by [. . .]."

If you are new, turn the question into a positive. "I started in February and I average two parties a week. I earn around

$[. . .] per party and I just signed my first recruit. We are both working toward a trip to Hawaii in October. Wouldn't it be great if you could come too? Here, let me show you . . ."

"I am earning $[. . .] a month and my goal is $[. . .]. To reach my goal, I have to do [. . .] presentations a week and find [. . .] motivated people."

★   If they ask, "How much does it cost?" they may be ready to sign but are concerned it may be too expensive.

Answer immediately, even if the question comes right at the outset. Never say, "I'll get to that later."

"You will be surprised. You pay just $250 for the basic starter kit or $500 if you want the fast-start kit. Here's what you get . . ."

When you weigh the cost of the kit against the benefits, we offer enormous value for money. Most people have to pay thousands of dollars to set up a business. Network marketing is an opportunity to start a business for peanuts.

★   Every objection is better out than in.

Frances: "I (or someone else) tried this before. It didn't work out."
You: "Tell me about it."

Many people test the waters with a company that doesn't work out before they find a fit. Learning about their experience will help you explain what's different about your business.

You: "I would guess around half of us have been with other companies before. I think it's important to find the right fit. The reason I chose this company is . . ."

★   How you respond when your prospect says, "I want to

think it over," may help you save the day. It could be a brush-off, but they may reconsider if you play your cards right.

> Anne: "Let me think about it."
>
> You: "Of course. It took me a couple of weeks to make up my mind because I wanted to be sure. This book/CD helped me answer a few questions I had about the business. I am over your way Wednesday and I can pick it up then."
>
> You may like to say, "You are right not to rush into a decision." Then in a relaxed voice, ask, "Is it the cost of the starter kit?"

If the prospect says yes, you have something to work on. If the prospect says no, you can probe further and find a solution to the sticking point.

When you are sure "no" means "no," thank prospects for their time and offer them a coupon redeemable for a generous discount off a future purchase. You have created a reason to call back in a couple of months and say, "I remembered the coupon I gave you and wondered if you wanted to redeem it? The specials this month are incredible."

★ Turn an objection into opportunity to reach the decision maker.

> Ellen: "I want to talk this over with my husband."
>
> You: "Good idea. There is no hurry to make a decision. Would you like me to come so I can answer any questions he may have?"

You may have a chance to get two people excited but don't move into convince mode. This business is not for everyone. No big deal. I've never fancied being a dentist, or a retailer, or an accountant, or a manufacturer.

★ Some prospects may be unsure about how network marketing or multilevel marketing works. A high-pressure sales pitch from a rogue representative of a legitimate network marketing company may have put them off.

> Dave: "Is this MLM?"
> You (expressed with enthusiasm): "Yes, it is. Have you been in multilevel marketing before?"
> Dave: "No. But a friend has."

You have been handed a golden opportunity to talk about your multilevel or network marketing business. Say, "Then let me explain what it is about."

If Dave answers, "yes," ask him, "What company?" and take it from there.

★ Occasionally, a question will be based on misinformation.

> Geoff: "Is this a pyramid scheme?"
> You: "No. Did you know pyramid schemes are illegal?"

Explain what a pyramid scheme is. "Pyramid schemes work on the 'greater fool' theory. People contribute money hoping for a big payoff if they can convince others to contribute. The rewards come from introducing others, rather than selling anything with real value. The earnings usually look too good to be true and that's because they are. Most of the people who get involved lose money."

Next, explain what network marketing is. "You can easily tell if a company is a legitimate network marketing company. Check that what you earn will be based on sales. Here's how our company works . . ."

★ Some people equate longevity with credibility.

> Matthew: "How long has the company been in business?"

Most companies include this information on the website and training manuals. If not, call them up or ask your sponsor.

If the company is new, say so:

"We are brand-new, but the founders have been in the industry
    for [. . .] years. It's exciting they have started a business that
    gives us a ground-floor opportunity. They really know what
    they are doing and it shows in the support we get."

★   Questions about legitimacy show your prospect is seriously considering your opportunity.

Geoff: "Are you a member of the Direct Selling Association
    (DSA)?"
You: "Yes, we are. Here is the logo." If your corporation is a
    member, the DSA logo will be on your literature and web-
    site.
"No, but we have applied and expect to be granted membership
    soon." Your company may be in the process of applying and
    it can take time to be confirmed.
"No, but . . ." If your company is not a member, it may be too
    small or too new to pay the dues, or it may belong to other
    reputable associations.

Keep in mind that it is not the objection, but the way you
handle it that counts. Learn to love questions and objections. If
your prospect is not communicating, the discussion—and your
chance of signing a new recruit—is over.

Above all, know that while you are interviewing your prospect, your prospect is interviewing you. The decision will be
influenced by how the person judges your professionalism, confidence, knowledge, and sincerity. When your confidence in your
business is unwavering, you will welcome all feedback.

PART IV

Are You a Recruiting Superstar?

CHAPTER THIRTY-THREE

Your Personal Recruiting Style

YOU NOW HAVE A WEALTH OF INFORMATION on how to become a recruiting superstar. It's time to see if you have what it takes to turn information into results. By comparing your personal recruiting style to the following recruiting profiles, you can test your potential to build a profitable downline organization.

You may discover strengths you can build on, and weaknesses you need to confront, to take advantage of the opportunities out there. You will also be empowered to help your new recruits recognize their strengths and weaknesses.

Recruiting Superstars

Recruiting superstars, the hottest of all recruiters, fall into one of the following profiles:

* Instinctive recruiter
* Intrepid recruiter

195

 ★ Intuitive recruiter

 ★ Influential recruiter

 ★ Inspired recruiter

Instinctive Recruiter

You believe in the business and have no qualms about approaching people you believe will benefit. You know what to do and you do it without hesitation. Recruiting is second nature to you, and you recruit consistently.

Intrepid Recruiter

You are determined, focused, and prepared to do whatever it takes to build your organization. You don't let setbacks spoil your chance of success. You live by the philosophy of "some will, some won't, so what, who's next!"

Intuitive Recruiter

You have great empathy with others. You can spot potential prospects at a hundred paces and you know how to push the right buttons to get them excited about the business.

Influential Recruiter

You are a natural leader. Charismatic and confident, you use your outstanding communication skills to present the business persuasively. Prospects are impressed by your strength and pleased you approached them.

Inspired Recruiter

You see yourself as an ambassador for the business. You are driven by a strong belief in the product and you love spreading the word. Prospects admire your strong convictions and loyalty to your brand.

If you have identified yourself as an instinctive, intrepid, intuitive, influential, or inspired recruiter, you are among the top 10 percent of recruiters. You are truly a recruiting superstar! Your business is growing, you achieve every recruiting incentive, and you are on target to reach your goals. You are the role model who sets the standard to which other network marketers aspire.

Superstars-in-the-Making

If you recognize yourself in one of the following profiles and you are willing to change, you definitely have what it takes to become a recruiting superstar.

- ★ Inquisitive recruiter
- ★ Impulsive recruiter
- ★ Idealist
- ★ Improviser
- ★ Incentive seeker

Inquisitive Recruiter

You are eager to learn as much as you can about recruiting. You read the manuals, invest in tapes, and buy books to fulfill your thirst for knowledge. You seek out role models, attend every training session, and are quick to seek advice from your sponsor.

Knowledge is always an advantage, but success won't come from the pages of a book. The best training comes on the job. Balance your desire to learn against the need to get out and practice recruiting at the front line.

Impulsive Recruiter

You recruit in short bursts before becoming distracted by something else. You have a wealth of underutilized talent and possibly you are disorganized.

The best recruiters in the business are consistent. Activity produces results, but you can't expect to get consistent results from inconsistent effort. Always have recruiting materials with you so that you are not caught unprepared. Paste notices on your planner, mirror, and fridge as a daily reminder of what you should be doing.

Idealist

You focus on product benefits at the expense of the business. You tend to look for fellow product fanatics and to be one-eyed about the qualities of your products compared with those of your competitors.

Although your loyalty is commendable, you run the risk of being seen as obsessive. You may also be tempted to exaggerate the benefits of your products. A team of sellers will reach more customers than a one-person crusader. If you want to build a profitable business, you must recruit.

Improviser

You are charismatic so you attract recruits, but you are a little on the lazy side. You adopt a casual approach to recruiting and you get by being charming.

Although your charm will take you so far, you owe it to your recruits to set an example they can follow. Stop taking shortcuts and do your homework on the company, the products, and the plan.

Incentive Seeker

You love carrots. It doesn't matter what they are, it's the thrill of winning that excites you. You work your business as a giant trophy hunt.

By all means go for the rewards, but realize your lack of stability will cost you in the long run if you do not invest in building relationships with the people you recruit. The best incentive should be a high, regular income. Shallow businesses do not have deep-enough foundations to survive long term.

If you identified yourself as an inquisitive, impulsive, idealist, improviser, or incentive-seeker, your strengths outweigh your weaknesses and you have a very real chance of moving into the top tier of recruiting superstars. Confront your weaknesses, and it will show in your results.

Low-Potential Recruiters

There is work to be done if you identify yourself in the recruiting profiles that follow. No doubt you are already frustrated by your lack of progress, but all is not lost. I could name many industry leaders whose businesses started to fly once they identified what was holding them back and worked to overcome it.

* Inefficient recruiter
* Indiscriminate recruiter
* Intimidated recruiter
* Inhibited recruiter
* Indecisive recruiter

Inefficient Recruiter

You leave a trail of forgotten promises and leads not followed up. Because your technique is on-again/off-again, when you do come across a likely prospect, you run the risk of losing the person.

It is time to shape up. You won't succeed in network marketing without a genuine interest in helping others. Your prospects deserve better than a recruiter who lacks self-discipline and personal management skills.

Indiscriminate Recruiter

You lack empathy. You approach prospects without discrimination, and without qualifying them, you launch into your pitch.

Although you may fool yourself that you are offering everyone an opportunity, in reality you are not taking the time to build rapport or to identify a genuine need.

It is time to get real. Not everyone is right for this business and you waste your time and theirs by taking an aggressive approach. Tone it down and try to develop a genuine interest in your prospects.

Intimidated Recruiter

You are overwhelmed at the recruiting aspect of the business. You fear rejection and you fear failure.

Although some doubts are natural, it takes courage to build a business. You may be surprised at how many seemingly confident network marketers will admit to feelings of inadequacy.

It is time to call an end to the pity party. The only way to overcome your self-doubts and your reluctance is to start approaching others. It's okay to admit to feeling apprehensive, but it's even better to stop focusing on yourself and start reaching out to people whose lives you could change if you gave them, and yourself, a chance.

Inhibited Recruiter

You can find a thousand reasons why you are not recruiting. Excuses are your forte, and you let outside influences distract you from your goals. You think, "I'm too [. . .], so don't expect me to [. . .]"

Make sure you aren't sabotaging your chance to build a great business by telling yourself that you aren't in control of your own life. You may not be able to control what happens to you, but you can certainly control how you respond to what happens.

Indecisive Recruiter

You have good intentions, but you don't ever get around to doing anything about them. Your prospect may decline your offer, but you'll never know if you waste time debating whether you should approach him or her. By the time you get around to making the approach, the prospect will probably have signed under someone else.

If you fall into the inefficient, indiscriminate, intimidated, in-hibited, or indecisive recruiter profile, don't be discouraged. You already know you're not getting results, but now you know it's not what other people are doing, but rather that your own atti-tudes and behaviors are holding you back. Think of it as a chance to change. Acknowledging your weaknesses is a positive step toward overcoming them.

Don't-Even-Think-About-It Recruiters

If you fall into these last two profiles, you have little or no busi-ness-building potential. It would take a miracle to get you re-cruiting.

* Indifferent recruiter
* Incapable recruiter

Indifferent Recruiter

You use the product but have zero interest in the business. You enjoy the products as a customer and perhaps even a wholesale buyer, but that's as far as it goes.

Incapable Recruiter

You lack the personal and social skills to be a business builder.

★ ★ ★ ★ ★ ★

Chances are you didn't see yourself in the indifferent or inca-pable profiles (or else why would you be reading this book?), but there is a lesson here. Don't waste time recruiting people who are better off as customers. Have the courage to recruit only people with whom you will be proud to associate. Bring the wrong peo-ple into your organization and you may frighten off promising candidates.

CHAPTER THIRTY-FOUR

Give Your New Recruits the Best Possible Start

FOR EVEN THE MOST CONSISTENT RECRUITERS, signing a new recruit is an exhilarating experience. It marks the beginning of your journey together, and you both hope it will be a long and mutually rewarding one.

Most new recruits start with an abundance of excitement and enthusiasm, but longevity comes from determination, drive, and discipline. You can't manufacture those qualities. That's up to your recruit.

Your role is to give your new recruits the training and support they need to succeed, especially at the outset.

Start by revisiting the goals they shared with you at the interview—what they want, when they want it, and how much they are prepared to do to get it. If the motivation for joining the business doesn't match the effort they are prepared to put in, something is going to have to change—the goal or the commitment.

Make sure your new recruits know you believe in them and will do everything you can to help, but that they are in control. Tell your recruits, "I know you can make a great success of this business and will give you the best support I can. But your success won't be due to anything I do. It will be due to what you do."

To ensure that your new recruits have the information and support they need when they most need it, I suggest you give them a copy of my book *Be a Network Marketing Superstar*. It will guide them step by step toward building a successful business. Not only will it inspire them to pursue their dreams, it will show them how.

The best compliment you can pay your new recruits is to believe in them, support them, and let them discover for themselves your belief was well placed.

☆　☆　☆　☆　☆

There are millions of prospects in the United States and now you know how to identify them. Apply the techniques you learned in this book, and you will soon build your six-figure income.

If you want it, and believe you deserve it, I know you can do it.

Index